KITCHEN

STYLES

ALLISON MURRAY MORRIS

CONSULTANT: ELLEN FRANKEL

PUBLICATIONS INTERNATIONAL, LTD.

Louis Weber, C.E.O.
Publications International, Ltd.
7373 North Cicero Avenue
Lincolnwood, Illinois 60646

Permission is never granted for commercial purposes.

Manufactured in the U.S.A.

8 7 6 5 4 3 2 1

ISBN: 0-7853-1274-9

Library of Congress Catalogue Card Number: 95-69633

ALLISON MURRAY MORRIS

CONSULTANT: ELLEN FRANKEL

Allison Murray Morris is former editor of *Woman's Day Kitchens & Baths, Woman's Day Home Decorating Ideas,* and *American HomeStyle Kitchen & Bath Planner.* She has covered the kitchen and bath industry extensively for both consumer and trade publications concentrating on home improvements and remodeling.

Ellen Frankel is former editor-in-chief of *1,001 Home Ideas* and former home-design editor of *McCall's.* She serves as consulting editor of home-furnishing features for several consumer publications. She is president of ECPM, Inc., editorial and marketing consultants specializing in the home-design field.

CONTENTS

PLANNING YOUR KITCHEN

Now more than ever, the old saying rings true: The kitchen is the heart of the home. These days, kitchens are so much more than places to prepare and eat meals. They're total living spaces where everything from bill paying to game playing takes place. Floor plans for new and remodeled kitchens often include such amenities as a custom entertainment center, a built-in desk, and casual dining space. Designers frequently incorporate the kitchen into a "Great Room," where kitchen, dining area, and living room are all part of one integrated living space for the family.

As a result, remodeling your kitchen (or designing a new one) involves much more than selecting cabinet finishes. Consider the amount of time you spend in the kitchen and what you do there. Do you spend hours lovingly preparing fabulous gourmet meals for your guests? Or do you cook and eat on the fly, using the microwave more often than the conventional oven? Perhaps your kids do their homework at the kitchen table while you get dinner ready. Or maybe you wish you had a spot in the kitchen for menu planning and bill paying. You and your family's needs must be taken into consideration when planning your kitchen.

Start by taking inventory of the kitchen you have right now. As we mentioned before, think about how you use your kitchen. Consider also how you think it will be used five years from now. Imagine the possibilities: Is there room for a stacked washer and dryer? What about a second sink or wall oven? Could you fit an island into the space? Some of these additions might seem ambitious to you at first, but keep in mind that upgrading a kitchen is an investment. If you're planning on staying in your home for a long time, you'll have many years to enjoy the fruits of your foresight. If you plan to sell your house in the next few years, try to calculate how much value your newly remodeled kitchen will add to your home.

You might also want to give some thought to a term you'll see from time to time in the pages that follow: the work triangle. The points of the work triangle are the refrigerator, range, and sink. If the work triangle is efficiently planned, it should make the kitchen convenient and easy to use by reducing the number of steps you take while you prepare a meal. Ideally, the work triangle should not be crossed by the traffic flow through the room.

And, of course, you'll want to give careful thought to how you'll decorate your kitchen. Picking up colors or motifs from other rooms will help tie the kitchen to the rest of the house, giving a pleasing feeling of continuity. Your kitchen will probably be in the same style as the rest of the rooms. For example, if you've decorated your living room in bold contemporary, your kitchen is unlikely to be in the traditional style. Whatever decorating style you choose,

remember that the most important person you have to please is yourself. As you sort through the myriad styles and kitchen fixtures, forget about the trends. Instead, focus on your own needs and preferences.

To help you with the sometimes daunting task of kitchen planning, *Kitchen Styles* offers a walking tour through more than 150 kitchens. The kitchens are divided into 11 categories by style. As you look around, jot down the things that appeal to you and those that don't. Don't worry if you find yourself picking out items from very different kitchens. Elements from several styles can be nicely combined. For example, if your house is filled with traditional furnishings, but you'd like a more modern decor in the kitchen, consider a soft contemporary style.

The kitchens showcased here are filled with great design ideas and creative solutions. Take your time and enjoy browsing through these attractive and well-planned rooms. They're sure to get you off to a good start in planning your own kitchen.

A COUNTRY CLASSIC

A variety of elements come together to make country kitchens cozy and inviting. Wood cabinets and wainscotting create a feeling of warmth. Unfitted or freestanding cabinets make the designs seem less reserved than contemporary kitchens. Open displays often use cookware for decoration, while architectural trim adds the finishing touch.

This kitchen features all of the above. Medium wood tones on the cabinets, floor, and wainscotting bring in a true country feel. Painted white cabinets add a more formal note to the oversize hutch, complete with slide-in range. Backsplash tiles feature Wedgewood-blue floral designs similar to the china collection displayed throughout the kitchen. Bare windows let sunlight flow freely in, welcoming yet more cheery warmth into this classically country kitchen.

COOK CENTER

Above: Hanging pots and pans are decorative and practical at the same time. White cabinets, along with blue and white tile, create a hutch behind the slide-in range. *Appliances: GE. Tile: Country Floors.*

DINING SPACE

Right: Bare windows and wainscotting are a classic backdrop for this dinette. Colorful pillows and decoration, like the miniature chair, are charming additions. *Designer: Jackie Naylor Interiors.*

SMALL SPACE

This kitchen may be narrow, but it's packed with storage and personality. Double raised panels, a hardwood floor, and trim along the counters give the space its natural appeal.

STARTING WITH COLLECTIBLES

You may not have to tear apart your existing kitchen to create the cozy country design you've been longing for. Take a look around; you might already have a country classic in the making. Rather than remodel her entire kitchen, the owner of this house used items she already owned.

Traditional cabinets were dressed up with new hardware. Some fresh paint here and there made the space look like new—and old. The design is filled with the homeowner's collection of antiques. Hardwood floors, molding, and wainscotting—often used in country motifs—enhance the antique country feel.

Dried cranberries offer a sparse window treatment that maximizes light flow through the kitchen's only window. Window treatments in the breakfast and dining rooms are also kept to a minimum to avoid distracting attention from the beautifully displayed antique accessories.

SIMPLE REDO

Above: Cosmetic changes helped old cabinets fit right into this kitchen's classic country decor. Look at what some new hardware and fresh paint can do. Designer: Sharon Matson.

DECORATIVE DETAILS

Left: Window treatments are kept to a minimum in this kitchen and breakfast room, but accessories such as baskets and dried flowers burst with color. The hanging bonnets are a wonderful old-time touch.

DINING ROOM

Right: Part of the home-owner's antique collection is displayed in the dining room. The painted wall, with chair-rail molding, offers a neutral backdrop.

A SUBTLE APPROACH

As appealing as classic country kitchens are, you might also find them to be very busy. Country designs are a reflection of personal taste not so much because of the colors and products included, but because of what's on display. Baskets or cookware sometimes hang from an overhead iron rail; dried flowers and pictures might ornament open shelves. Family heirlooms and fine antiques can find their way from living room to kitchen.

This design shows just how uncluttered a classic country kitchen can be. Traditional raised-panel cabinets keep utensils and cookware out of view. Cabinet fronts give the appliances a built-in look. One focal point is the double glass-front cabinets, reminiscent of classic furniture pieces, that showcase the homeowners' ceramic collection. The bare bay window is another attraction.

Nooks alongside the cooking area and above the refrigerator are also spots for display and storage. Everywhere, the displayed items are in full view but out of the way, creating a clean, open country look.

SMALL SPACE

A creative plan fits in all the necessary components of a kitchen, along with an informal breakfast bar and decorative storage.
Tile: Country Floors. Island countertop: DuPont Corian.

GOURMET STYLE

With its commercial range and freestanding work island, this kitchen is a serious cook's delight. The stainless double sink and adjacent countertop fit right in.

LIGHT & AIRY COUNTRY

It's no wonder that country kitchens have become so popular. They're filled with sunlight and colorful fabrics. The decorative woodwork dresses up the room and helps it blend with the rest of a country-style home. Painted accents and glass-fronted cabinets allow the homeowner to enhance and display a treasured china collection. The result is a practical, attractive kitchen that really feels like home.

If you're planning a country kitchen, start with lightly stained cabinets to show off the wood's natural grain and make the space appear roomier. (If something darker is your pleasure, lighten up the rest of the decor.) Add a large window or bright backsplash in brick, tile, or paint. In this country kitchen, commercial-style products, including a range and stainless steel counters, lend a gourmet touch. And to top it off, don't forget to add an area rug for softness underfoot.

PERSONAL TOUCHES

Above: Traditional cabinets and a wild bird motif bring natural elegance to this country kitchen. The glass cabinets are stepped around a pass-through into an adjoining room. Cabinets: Chapman House. Faucet: Kohler. Artistic painting: Michael Pawlowski.

BREAKFAST ROOM

Right: What a place to start the day! Cozy cushions and white cabinets create a sunlit seat. The rustic tile floor blends with the adjacent kitchen. Designers: Carolyn Bailey Durbin and Nancy McGowen, Allied ASID. Fabric: Brunschwig & Fils.

COOKING CENTER

With pots hanging from antique beams overhead, this massive island is a chef's dream. A commercial-style range and undercounter wall oven team up with storage drawers and smooth work surfaces. *Designer: Franco Nonahal, Architect. Range: Viking.*

A CLASSIC RESTORATION

How do you put a modern kitchen into an older space without destroying the room's antique appeal? This classic country kitchen shows the way. Located in one of its community's oldest homes, the room used to be a barn. The starting point of the renovation project was the existing beams—original to the home.

The white cabinets are fresh and new, but their traditional design suits the wainscotted surroundings. The rustic decor, however up-to-date, is timeless. Tile floors and butcher block counters can withstand lots of kitchen activity and, as they wear, they'll only become more charming. With a large center island and a mix of modern amenities, this kitchen is a treat for gourmet cooks as well as for antique lovers.

BUILT-INS

Above: Custom cabinets make a furniture-like hutch for dinnerware and colorful ceramics. Wine is neatly tucked inside the island, while baskets and shiny copper cookware are in full view.

NEW DESK

Left: This country kitchen may have a traditional decor, but its features are all up-to-date. The built-in desk is a popular addition to kitchens.

TURN OF THE CENTURY

Old homes have a certain ambience and style that many newer designs try to emulate, with more or less success. If you have an old home, consider all the alternatives before you demolish the kitchen. It may contain items you would later regret discarding.

This country kitchen is 100 years old. Although it's been given a fresh look with new cabinets, counters, and all the latest in technology, the kitchen's architectural elements—such as the double crown molding—point back to its history. Brass pulls on the white cabinets contrast with the much darker wood floor for a fully classic look. All the elements come together to carry on the classic spirit of this historic kitchen.

DINING AREA

Right: New traditional base cabinets are topped with a refurbished hutch in this floor-to-ceiling arrangement found in the adjacent dining area. Cabinets: Brubaker Kitchens.

COOKING CENTER

Below: One highlight of the kitchen is its copper-like range hood and commercial-style range. The gas cooktop and counter are just a turn away. Designer: Merrie Fredericks/NKBA Design Competition 1993. Range: Garland. Ventilation: KitchenAid.

FRESH GOOD LOOKS

What a difference a fresh coat of paint can make! If you want to update your kitchen and dining room but aren't sure about what you want, try a change of color. You'll notice a big difference in the look and feel of the room. Best of all, this makeover can fit almost any budget.

There are plenty of other inexpensive ways to make your kitchen reflect your personality. Put a favorite collection on display so you can enjoy it. Cover the dinette chairs with a striking color you never thought you'd use inside your home. The two rooms shown here are great examples of the magic you can work with a little imagination.

One note of caution: Do think before you paint. You don't want to do something you'll regret once the paint has dried. The joy of creating a new look will wear off if you have to do it over again and again to get the color right.

DINING ROOM

Below: Striking colors bring good cheer to this dining area. The painted designs, wood table, and large brick fireplace and mantel are all staples of country design.

ON DISPLAY

Right: From the hand-painted cabinets and simple door hardware to the miniature chair collection on display, this kitchen is filled with personality. The butcher-block counter and multicolored floor add to the rustic charm. Designer: Alvin Schneider.

SCENES FROM ABROAD

An apothecary chest isn't something typically found in a kitchen. The kitchen shown here, however, is rather extraordinary. The center island/pharmaceutical cabinet, a Swedish import, is just one of the European treasures that influence the room's style.

A round light fixture, reminiscent of those hung outside shops in France, adds a quaint touch above the island. Beautifully carved tiled molding tops the cooking area. There's also an interesting storage nook filled with porcelain drawers and canisters for sugar and spices. The containers have Swedish and German origins.

To match the eclectic mix of European imports, new cabinetry was custom finished to look slightly aged; delicate relief carvings add a personal touch. Tile and French limestone add soft hues to floors and countertops, completing the charming mix of old and new, European and American.

CLASSIC IMPORTS

Above: Sugar, coffee, and the like are stored in antique storage drawers from Germany. A double row of Swedish canisters keeps spices accessible. Designer: Jackie Warschaw. Stylist: Donna Pizzi.

WORK ISLAND

Left: Swedish pharmacy drawers are the base of this large center island. The island provides open counterspace and a traditional sink, the kitchen's second.

COOKING AREA

Right: Commercial cooking appliances are tucked into a tile surround and topped with elegant molding. A colorful collection of pitchers is displayed overhead. Refrigerator: Traulsen. Range: Wolf.

OLD-WORLD ELEGANCE

Not too many homeowners would shed tears over a kitchen that's too big! But large kitchens do present unique challenges, including keeping frequently used appliances and products close together and making a large space warm and welcoming.

In order to make this massive kitchen cozier and more practical, the designer divided it into sections for working, sitting, and dining. In the working area, a mix of finishes and materials blends together to visually soften the large room. Traditional cabinets are painted crisp white. Tile has a warm, washed look. The center island, with mullion glass doors, has a hardworking marble top. On windows, foliage takes the place of heavy window treatments.

The design is filled with European country touches, starting with the plate rails and decorative molding. Old-World accents like these add just the right decorative note to this cozy, inviting space.

BUILT-IN BAR

Above: Classic wine racks are set above a marble top in this pretty bar set-up. Open shelving is popular in country kitchens. Designer: Designs by Florence Perchuk, Ltd. Cabinets: Wood-Mode.

CENTER ISLAND

Right: Wall cabinets are used in the island base to keep dinnerware within closer reach. The marble-topped island serves as a partial divider between the main kitchen and eating area. Sinks and fittings: Kohler.

CUSTOM DETAILS

Left: From its painted air balloon tiles to the decorative plate rails and molding, this roomy kitchen is designed to be comfortably inviting. Cooktop: KitchenAid.

NATURALS WARM UP

Mixing natural materials is a great way to give your kitchen a unique look. The challenge is making the materials work with, rather than against, each other. In this kitchen wood, limestone, and marble come together harmoniously. The result is a sparkling classic that's packed with modern conveniences.

Everywhere you turn, there's something interesting to catch your eye. Ornamental carved details and furniture-like cabinet arrangements add a European flavor. The center island, complete with accompanying pastry table, is one focal point. Just a few feet away, a commercial cooktop creates another focal point. Surrounded by marble and limestone diamonds that complement the countertops and floor, it incorporates a mix of materials. Cookware is displayed below in an accessible cut-out with ornate columns, rope molding, and carved rosettes. The hood is painted to resemble the limestone and marble used in the kitchen.

LIKE FURNITURE

Below: With a hand-rubbed look, green cabinetry stands out among its darker counterparts. The piece is multifunctional—with a built-in pantry, broom closet, and audio/video entertainment system. Cabinets: Hallmark Cabinets.

CENTER ISLAND

Right: A freestanding pastry table offers additional workspace adjacent to the island. Two custom-made fixtures lend an interesting design element and task lighting. Designer: Gary E. White, CKD, CBD. Cooktop: Thermador. Custom liner and fan: Vent-A-Hood.

FOR FAMILY LIVING

It's easy to see why kitchens like this one are often called the heart of the home. The family-style plan is wide open, while still featuring separate task areas. There's a marble-topped food prep island with dropped butcher block, easily accessible to kids. Built in alongside the wall ovens, a desk can be used by all members of the household. And a full range of modern appliances is available for the cook.

The kitchen design is inspired by European craftsmanship. The heavily carved vent hood, above a commercial-style range, features a floral motif. The tile backsplashes bring the floral motif to colorful life, while the mural behind the cooktop adds another vibrant accent.

RANGE HOOD

Above: Rich carvings turn the range hood into a work of art. Precise and colorful tile designs spruce up all the room's backsplashes. The painted design imitates the hood decoration. Designer: Franco Nonahal. Builder: Bob Pulte. Custom tilework: Debra Hecht.

CUSTOM CABINETS

Left: Moldings and trim are stained to match the custom cabinets. From the doors to the porcelain hardware, their look is pure country. European apothecary drawers add storage nooks to the wall cabinets. Cabinets: Downsview Cabinetry.

TWO-TIERED ISLAND

Right: The kids can spend time coloring or snacking while a parent prepares dinner at this multipurpose island. Wine and other essentials are stored underneath the counters. Range and ovens: Viking.

SHADES OF BLUE

Remodeling a kitchen doesn't necessarily mean tearing out cabinets and changing the floor plan. This kitchen was classic 1950s, right down to the brown tile floor, before its makeover. Out went the wallcoverings, floor, and countertops. The cabinets were so sturdy, though, and the layout so functional that the homeowner and designer decided to keep them. After some stripping, painting, and glazing, the cabinets were revitalized in shades of blue.

Now the kitchen has European elegance—from its railed vent hood to the Victorian chandelier. A grandfather clock contributes another period detail. Muted blue tiles with colorful bands running from side to side look as soft as carpeting. The counters are seamless in solid surfacing and feature a rounded edge treatment.

BREAKFAST BAR

Below: Equally appealing and functional, this two-tiered island offers a comfortable work surface and a dropped counter to accommodate chairs instead of stools. The light fixture is classic Victorian. Designer: Sharon M. Pretto, ISID. Countertops: Nevamar. Chandelier: Barnette Shure.

GOURMET SET-UP

Right: The restaurant-style cooking area will meet the needs of any cook. Two pairs of wall ovens and an extensive cooktop are within steps of the spacious work counter. Decorated tile and rails for hanging cookware create a pretty backdrop. Wallpaper and fabrics: Hanson & Co. Tile: Nemo Tile. Refrigerator: Sub-Zero.

A TASTE OF FRANCE

Some country kitchens are just a little different. This kitchen is a good example. While molding does add a decorative element, no painted tile dresses up the counter edges and backsplash. The look is minimal; the appliances are stainless. In the end, though, it all comes together in a kitchen that looks as though it was lifted from a small town in France.

A striking use of green gives the simple traditional cabinets a fresh look. An antique-look pastry table is used as a primary work area; the marble top is ideal for working with dough. Side-by-side windows let natural light flow freely into the space. Additional light comes from the ornate metal fixture hanging from the ceiling.

The kitchen's French country flavor is enhanced by quaint touches like the baskets that pull out between the range and refrigerator and the faux shutters above the indoor flower garden. It's a look that just says, *"Bon appétit!"*

EXTRA WORKSPACE

Left: This French pastry table lends European charm, while playing a vital role. The layout may be limited but the cook has ample space to prepare meals and sweet temptations.

COUNTRY CHARM

Although the range, hood, and refrigerator look rather commercial, this kitchen is filled with cozy country touches. The pastry table, narrow baskets, and decorative chandelier are examples. Designer: Jackie Naylor Interiors, Inc. Refrigerator: Traulsen. Range: Viking. Range hood: Best.

PAINTED TOUCHES AND PINE

Hand-painted tile is a frequent and welcome feature in country kitchens. Although almost anything goes, florals and barnyard animals are popular because of their vivid colors. This delightful design teams decorated tile in both motifs with knotty pine cabinets. Wood molding and a custom hood, both staples of European country designs, complete the warm rustic setting.

Central to the design, a large island works as a food preparation area, within easy reach of the cooktop and the sink. A warming oven and extra storage are located below its accented tile top.

And speaking of storage, this kitchen would delight any cook with its abundant cabinet space. There's even a semi-private nook with specialty cabinets for wine and glassware. This is truly a kitchen for connoisseurs of both cooking and style.

FOOD PREPARATION

Opposite: This center island is easily accessed from the double sink and cooktop. Wood details, like the beaded end panels and feet, are pure country. Designer: Sharon Overstake, CKD. Cabinetry and hood: Wm. Ohs, Inc.

CUSTOM DETAILS

Below: A colorful rooster and other decorations painted onto white tile create a bright backdrop in this warm pine kitchen. The cooktop was lowered to make room for the custom European hood and tile art. Cooktop and ovens: Dacor. Tile designs: Lisa Burt.

VISION IN WHITE

Old-world charm is the key to this kitchen's appeal. Ornate fretwork, open shelves, and plate racks all contribute to its Euro-country feel. Although all the cabinets flow from one to the next, each combination has a specific purpose and unique look. For example, a hutch near the table and chairs doubles as a display case for colorful ceramics.

The white kitchen is formal, yet welcoming. The fabrics, with foliage and grape patterns, and the floor, with bold diamonds, are carefree. The peninsula offers a place for the cooktop and casual seating, while the separate eating area provides a more formal environment for dining. Decorative moldings and custom woodwork give the cabinets the appeal of fine furniture. Direct lighting from the valance brightens the counter below.

Below: With slots for daily messages and mail, a desk like this one can be a blessing in a family kitchen. Two tiers on one side are angled for a more decorative look facing into the rest of the kitchen.
Designer: Bob Howering. Cabinets: Rutt Custom Kitchens.

GREAT ROOM

Left: Formal and informal dining areas meet up in this open layout. The white country cabinets and new appliances are warmed up with lively fabrics, tall windows, and other living room touches.

A SOFTER SIDE OF GREEN

Green has come a long way in interior design since the days of avocado. Lately green is showing up all over, especially in kitchens. A washed green gives this kitchen much of its personality. It's such a neutral shade that all the other colors in the design, from the classic wood tones to the florals, blend right in.

Natural wood floors, full-frame cabinets, and pretty painted tiles—like those pictured here—are common in country kitchens. The European accents in this design are most notable in the detailed backsplash. Fruit, florals, and bread are colorfully depicted, giving a cozy, Old-World feel.

The kitchen is as hardworking as it is attractive. Distance between the appliances is close enough for comfort, yet large enough for a clean, uncluttered look. A fold-down butcher-block counter extension expands the workspace. The continuous wood floor unifies the areas, while the small peninsula creates a separation between kitchen and eating area. The pairing of looks and practicality makes this a great kitchen for entertaining and casual dining.

BACKSPLASH MURAL

Below: Painted tiles and light green cabinetry give this kitchen a lot of personality. The full-frame cabinets are pure country, while the vivid mural has European influences. Designer: Alvin Schneider Design. Refrigerator: GE.

EATING IN

Right: By extending the layout, the designer fit in a dinette and additional cabinets. The bright blue hutch and fold-down butcher-block are nice finishing touches.

COOKING CENTER

Elaborate gourmet meals can be prepared at this heavy-duty range and countertop set-up, both housed under a double-molded and hand-carved hood.
Designer: Beverly Ellsley. Range: Thermador.

CUSTOM-CARVED DETAILS

This unusual kitchen looks more like a work of art than a workspace. Ornate carvings turn the cabinets and molding into sculpted masterpieces. The cabinet arrangements themselves resemble finely crafted European furniture. And yet, this ornate, formal kitchen is still very comfortable and functional.

The word "elaborate" sums up the cooking area, complete with professional-looking range and floating hood. Vines and grapes adorn the hood's rim. Lightly veined salmon marble countertops offer ample workspace. The built-in casual breakfast area is dressed up with a colorful brocade fabric. Other colorful accents include the dried flowers and diamonds on the white tile floor.

Not everyone has the space, time, or budget for this kitchen, but keep in mind that just one or two well-executed carved patterns can add European flair to any kitchen.

MARBLE ISLAND

Above: An oven, dishwasher, and integral sink all find a home in this large center island. Masterful wood detailing turns the island and other cabinets into pieces of formal furniture. *Sink: Kohler. Fittings: The Broadway Collection.*

EATING IN

Left: Bench-style seating surrounds an iron and blue glass table in this informal dining area. Mirror and wood meet on refrigerator fronts, making the large appliances seem less cumbersome. *Cabinets: Beverly Ellsley Collection. Fabric: Fronthill. Refrigerator: Sub-Zero.*

BRINGING THE OUTSIDE IN

Much like those found in southern France, lavish gardens and patios surround the exterior of this crisp kitchen. French doors bring the colors and fragrances in from the yard.

The white decor is very formal, with a contemporary flair. Open shelving and leaded glass make attractive display cases for a decorative dinnerware collection. Blue, yellow, and various other lively colors on the scenic backsplash tile are a nice contrast to the counters and cabinets.

The beautiful center island, complete with second sink, serves many purposes. Ideally located for food preparation, its generous size also makes it a perfect work area for cutting and arranging flowers.

GARDEN ROOM

French doors lead from the kitchen to elegant gardens blooming with color. Inside, leaded glass doors keep decorative porcelain pieces in full view.

SEPARATE STATIONS

Left: A spacious layout enabled the designer to plan distinct work areas, including a sit-down desk and roomy island. The island is suitable for preparing food, entertaining guests, and pursuing hobbies. Designer: Kulla Kitchens. Cabinets: Heritage Customer Kitchens.

BASKET OF DELIGHTS

From its richly antiqued cabinets to its ornate range hood, this lovely kitchen overflows with European country charm. A pretty picnic basket, complete with bouquet, loaf of French bread, and bottle of red wine, is painted on the tiles behind the cooktop. Topped with a custom two-tone hood and carved molding, the colorful mural sets the tone for the whole kitchen. Painted floral tiles—a hallmark of country kitchens—are a bright accent on the white tile counters and backsplash.

The cabinets are a traditional mix of sizes, shapes, and styles, including glass front, raised panels, and open shelves. The cabinet doors sport smoky blue accents. The kitchen is flooded with light by the over-the-counter greenhouse window, adding to the cheerful country feel. Tambour doors keep appliances out of view. A freestanding table, like those often found in European kitchens, provides centrally located work space. This space lets its owner cook with all the modern conveniences while enjoying the quaint atmosphere of an Old World kitchen.

TWO SINKS

The main sink is illuminated by natural light. A second sink, in the peninsula, works overtime when the homeowner is entertaining or getting help preparing meals. Designers: Maria Weingard and David L. Schneider. Cabinets: Rutt Custom Kitchens.

A GARDEN-LOVER'S KITCHEN

This kitchen is as warm and welcoming as the yard it overlooks. Traditional honey pine cabinets bring country charm to the L-shape plan. White floor tiles and solid surfacing counters are a neutral, yet striking, contrast. The decor is enhanced by tile on the walls and a greenhouse window above the sink.

The center island takes full advantage of the spacious room. The round sink serves as a preparation sink for entertaining, and the built-in wine storage is an added convenience. An open traffic plan helps keep the space carefree and practical. Sunlight flows freely into the atrium-style breakfast area.

A corridor, which isn't shown, runs adjacent to the kitchen and facilitates the homeowners' horticultural interests. Built-in cabinetry, counterspace, and an oversized sink let them pursue their hobby year-round.

DOUBLE SINK

Above: A clean look is achieved around the practical double-bowl sink by undermounting it in the solid surfacing countertop. Herbs and small flowering plants thrive in the greenhouse window. Sink and faucet: Franke. Countertop: Wilsonart. Fabrics and wallcoverings: Waverly.

BUILT-IN LOOK

Left: Cabinet panels help conceal the refrigerator and make it seem less cumbersome. Designer: Kulla Kitchens. Interior Design Consultant: Malcolm Eisenberg. Cabinets: Heritage Custom Kitchens. Refrigerator/Freezer: Sub-Zero.

CENTER ISLAND

Right: This spacious island gets high marks for style. The granite top and high-back seats are both attractive and functional. Countertop: Marble Crafters. China and accessories: Tiffany & Co.

A NICE BLEND OF STYLES

If you're thinking of blending country and contemporary styles, let this kitchen show you how. Country elements fit right into a clean-lined modern setting to create an appealingly harmonious mix.

Traditional cabinets usually lend themselves to country designs. But when they're painted up-to-date white and topped with glistening grayish natural stone, the cabinetry changes its outlook. The addition of white-on-white appliances and decorative panels promotes a contemporary, fully built-in look. On the floor, a classic checkerboard pattern is lightened up to offer a neutral mix of contemporary and country.

STORAGE

Above: Who couldn't use an extra tall cabinet just for glasses and dinnerware? With less depth than a typical base or wall cabinet, these shelves hold plenty at an easy-to-reach distance.

DOUBLE SINKS

Right: If space permits, a double sink can come in quite handy. The window and glass cabinet door designs are country; the white-on-white appliances are contemporary.

ISLAND "L"

Traffic is directed through this kitchen by the L-shape island, which also divides the main kitchen space from the eating area. *Designer: Barbara Hauben Ross. Consultant: Abbey's Kitchens & Baths.*

BURNISHED WOOD FROM HEAD TO TOE

A kitchen that opens to a family room and separate dining space can be wonderful. But it takes careful planning to create a kitchen that stands on its own, yet blends harmoniously with the adjacent rooms. This well-designed kitchen meets the challenge head on.

The burnished wood cabinets and wood plank ceiling could just as easily be part of a country home. With a dramatic skylight and totally built-in look, however, the design is given a contemporary edge. All the new appliances are customized with front panels to match the traditional recessed cabinets. Blue gingham at the windows and tiles on the counter and backsplash add some extra country touches.

The angled peninsula is essential to the kitchen's functional layout. Here, a gas cooktop anchors the main work triangle. Two stools pull up for informal dining or enjoyable conversation with the cook. The dining area nearby is perfect for family meals and entertaining.

BUILT-IN LOOKS

Below: Front panels on the appliances give this country kitchen a contemporary built-in look. Designer: Joe LaMantia, CKD, and Lynn Larsen, CKD. Appliances: KitchenAid.

DINING AREA

Right: Walls of glass surround a more formal eating area adjacent to the kitchen. The peninsula, drenched with sunlight from the skylight above, is reserved for quick snacks. Cabinets: Heritage Custom Kitchens. Tile: Kolormatte.

CABINETS OF DISTINCTION

Wood cabinets are a feature in most country kitchens. Sometimes they're stained; sometimes they're painted. Nowadays, cabinets that show off wood's natural grain—irregularities and all—are popular. The two kitchens showcased here let their wood cabinets make a statement, keeping decorative trim and molding to a minimum.

Turquoise paint was carefully applied and wiped to give the kitchen on the right an aged appeal. The farmhouse-style cabinets are accented with simple wood knobs. The rich hardwood floor is dramatic underfoot and makes the space appear larger. Stainless appliance fronts add a modern touch. Tile counters complete the contemporary rustic look.

Natural cabinets add warmth and charm to the kitchen below. Bright counter and backsplash tiles are an interesting contrast. A contemporary accent comes into the country kitchen with built-in appliances. Custom panels help the refrigerator and dishwasher blend right in.

CENTER ISLAND

Left: Bleached wood cabinets and floors are dressed up with bright tiles on the counters and backsplash. The back of the island is raised to create a private niche for the cooktop. Designers: Sara L. Reep, CKD, ASID, and Carolyn Haney. Cabinets: Fieldstone.

OLD IS NEW

Right: Free from ornate trim and molding, this design is more contemporary than many country kitchens. The aged cabinets and rich wood floor are a rustic combination. Designer: Albert Fink, Ph.D., CKD. Cabinets: Thekla Cabinetry, Inc.

WITH ACCENTS OF BLUE

Country kitchens use countless details to evoke the feeling of years gone by. Sometimes the look is subtle; other times it's not. A taste of early Americana vibrates through this showhouse kitchen.

Pine cabinets bring in the traditional wood look so often found in country classics. But the design is given a more contemporary feel with crisp solid surfacing counters and a lightly patterned resilient floor. The designer also stayed away from the heavy moldings and trimwork so common in country designs.

The kitchen includes a nice mix of old and new. Out of view, the refrigerator is painted to resemble an antique armoire. The old-fashioned drop-in sink coordinates with a collection of fine china. The modern appliances next to the sink harmonize with the room's colors. Using the best of both worlds, this kitchen shows how country can go contemporary without losing its charm.

UP-TO-DATE

Left: Although the sink is a classic, the vinyl floor, dishwasher, and trash compactor are modern amenities. The cabinets and arched faucet are pure country. *Countertop: Avonite. Sink and faucet: Kohler.*

COOKING CENTER

Right: A double wall oven and adjacent cooktop fit into this compact area. Backed by brick, the center also includes a drawer for pots and pans. *Designer: Nancy Mullan. Cabinets: Wood-Mode.*

FILLED WITH LIGHT

Cabinets have a big influence on a kitchen's style. Glossy black lacquer just isn't going to work in a country kitchen. Traditional white cabinets like those shown here, on the other hand, can fit into almost any setting. Here, they help create a contemporary country look.

The open plate display above the sink is a country decoration, as are the moldings and framed window. The wood floor also contributes to the country setting. Glistening dark countertops and the kitchen's fully built-in look are more contemporary features, along with the breakfast bar. Large windows and recessed lights make the whole space feel brighter. And, pulling it all together, the white cabinets with country styling smooth the transition between two styles.

TRIPLE WINDOW

Below: There's quite a view from the double-bowl sink. An undressed window and recessed ceiling lights keep the work areas well lighted.
Designer: Anne Mullin Interiors, Inc.

WORK TRIANGLE

Right: A built-in gas cooktop, set in this roomy island, completes the work triangle. By extending the countertop, the designer made room for a relaxed dining area in the kitchen.

JEWEL TONES SPARKLE

EXTRA STORAGE

Below: Storage galore is offered in rustic-looking country cabinets, including those in the center island. Painted cabinets add a handcrafted touch while accenting the pine's natural appeal.

Nothing shows off the grain of wood cabinetry like a good finishing job or, better yet, two contrasting finishes. The first thing you'll notice in these two kitchens is the homey painted jewel-tone cabinetry. But your attention will probably quickly move to the beautifully stained woods used elsewhere in the designs.

In the kitchen on the right, a contemporary vaulted ceiling is decorated with rustic beams stained a dark shade to match the floor. The cabinets are oak with a green finish; the floor, countertop, and beams have a bordeaux finish. The kitchen below has pine cabinets that brighten the space with tones of blue and yellow-brown while providing plenty of storage. In both kitchens, the designers created more contemporary versions of country kitchens by keeping decorative moldings and open storage to a minimum.

OPEN AND AIRY

Right: A massive half-wall of window drenches this kitchen with sunlight. The striking design is contemporary, while the painted recessed cabinets, open shelves, and beaded panels are classic country.
Designer: Steven P. Emerson.
Cabinets: Rutt.

MIXING THE ELEMENTS

Personal preferences are the most important factor in creating a kitchen design. That's why so many kitchens combine elements from more than one design style. It's also why kitchens are so interesting to look at! What one homeowner might use in a country kitchen, another would buy to accent a retro design.

This kitchen has a country flavor with contemporary touches to lighten up the decor. The dramatic ceiling, from which a neutral light fixture hangs, is more modern than classic. The island mimics the shape and size of the ceiling cutout, but not its style. Country seating, a hardwood floor, and a built-in hutch give just the right touch of country to this contemporary/rustic blend.

Right: Visitors to this kitchen will certainly look skyward. The large ceiling cutouts bring a contemporary edge to the country design. *Designer: Val Siddell.*

Left: Oak is dressed up with white accents on the counters, appliances, and walls. Informal seating fits three at the island near the separate table and chairs. *Cabinets: Crestwood.*

CONCRETE AND STEEL WITH A TWIST

Neither concrete nor stainless steel are materials that most homeowners choose to expose in their kitchens. But the goal here was to match the kitchen to its house, which is made of these two nearly indestructible products. This kitchen was designed for a modern art and furniture enthusiast. The idea was to create a space that was sleek, simple, and bare: a truly contemporary kitchen.

An ultramodern peninsula is the focal point of the design. Its acid-washed granite counter floats on polished steel posts. While the cook prepares food, his guests can sit along the counter.

Although the design might be considered cold, it's actually warmed by easy-to-use features. The homeowner, who entertains often, chose exposed storage under the gas cooktop. Pots and pans are always in view and very accessible. An underfoot heating system literally warms up the floor. And custom accessories mounted on the backsplash keep counterspace free from clutter. Along with the hanging halogen spotlights, these practical touches contribute to the boldly contemporary decor.

EXTRA STORAGE

Above: This crisp white kitchen is packed with storage space, including open racks below the cooktop for pots and pans.

SEAMLESS DESIGN

Above: Built-in good looks are achieved with an integral stove top and double-bowl sink in the stainless steel counter. The backsplash supports a cutting board and knife rack.

CONCRETE FLOOR

Left: Glazing on the concrete floor makes it look more appealing for interior applications. The naturally cool surface is warmed by a radiant hydronic heating system. Designer: Cecilia Campa. Architect: Jan Fillinger.

RAISED PENINSULA

Left: With steel supports and backdrop, the raised peninsula looks like it's floating. Guests seated at the contemporary counter can converse with the cook. Refrigerator: Sub-Zero.

MAKING A STATEMENT

L ustrous materials. Built-in appliances and cabinets. Modern decor without frills. This kitchen typi-
fies what contemporary styling is all about.

   With no protruding door hardware, cabinets upon cabinets flow without visual interruption.
Horizontal stripes running across one wall of cabinets create a light-and-dark contrast. The lighter
stripe color dominates the main sink area. Black granite counters, speckled with color, are equally
elegant and hardworking. Everywhere, surfaces are smooth and lines flow in a space that is the soul
of contemporary style.

BUILT-INS

*Left: Decorative panels
conceal the refrigerator so
that it blends right in with
the cabinets. The stylish
radiant cooktop and integral
sink turn the center island
into a complete work area.*
Designer: Ken Neuman.

SHAPELY ISLAND

*Right: The island's unique
shape, done with rich cabinets and a dark solid top,
takes center stage in this
modern kitchen design.*

A ROOM WITH A VIEW

If your kitchen offers a view of the great outdoors, your plan is already off to a good start. Whether it overlooks a sunny family garden, ocean, or golf course, a kitchen with a natural backdrop can be something special. Of course, the trick is to make the kitchen look as good as the property it overlooks.

Black, white, and stainless create a contemporary flavor in this design. And because the color scheme is not commonly found in nature, there's no competition between the sleek kitchen and the green backyard.

The plan contains many interesting features. The island's two levels create a suitable spot for casual dining and food preparation. Extra-long horizontal cabinet pulls match the shiny stainless appliance fronts. A countertop runs the length of the window wall, creating ample workspace.

PRACTICAL ISLAND

Right: An inlaid black stripe accents the counter edge while playing up the kitchen's contrasting color scheme. The two-tiered island has one side for creating culinary masterpieces and another for eating them. Solid surfacing: DuPont Corian.

STEPPING UP

Staggered cabinets highlight the commercial-style range and vent hood while adding a decorative spot for storing glasses. The modern window design fills the space with natural light and a real-life mural. Designers: Gary Hancock and Deborah Litz-Beard. Hood: Best. Range: Thermador.

CENTERED AROUND THE FAMILY

This kitchen, like many of its updated counterparts, is designed with a whole family in mind. The informal dining island allows plenty of space for a family of five to enjoy a meal together, do homework, or just socialize. A built-in television and separate desk area (not seen in these photos) help make the kitchen a multipurpose family room.

From its white frameless cabinets to a stunning reverse coffer above the island, the kitchen is a dramatic modern variation of the traditional L-shape design. The curvaceous design is not only up-to-date but practical. The main components—cooktop, sink, double oven, and dishwasher—are within steps of each other. The refrigerator stands nearby, on the opposite side of the island. The white solid surfacing counters keep traffic flowing right along. Added features include two integral sinks and a drainboard routed alongside the main sink.

WORK ISLAND

Left: A second sink and adjacent counterspace create a spacious food preparation area. Stainless steel trivet rods, on either side of the cooktop, keep hot pots off the white solid surfacing countertop. Designer: Gary White, CKD.

BREAKFAST BAR

A family of five can enjoy casual dining without getting in the way of the cook. The suspended light fixture and vent hood are practical, contemporary elements.

DESIGNED FOR TWO COOKS

A lot of contemporary ideas liven up this teal and bleached wood kitchen, in addition to its up-to-date color scheme. Cabinets are staggered for comfort and aesthetics. The island displays cuts reminiscent of modern architecture. And custom panels on appliances lend an integral feel.

The contemporary look suits the owners' contemporary lifestyle. With both spouses working outside the home, meal planning and preparation have become more of a group effort. Whether kids or a spouse help out at dinner, a practical design includes separate work areas. This kitchen is designed with "his" and "her" sides, unified by the center island. The space is ample enough to fit two dishwashers, two microwaves, and two sinks, in addition to a cooktop, built-in oven, refrigerator, and pantry. In this generous and comfortable kitchen, family members can use all phases of meal preparation to catch up with each other as they cook.

TWO COOKS

Above: Designed with "his" and "her" food prep areas, this kitchen has two walls of cabinets and appliances separated by a sit-down island. Only one of the walls is visible here. Designers: Jim Krengel, CKD, CBD, ISID, and Rina Cohen, MDIA. Sinks and faucets: American Standard.

STAGGERED HEIGHTS

Right: Raising the oven has several advantages, such as minimizing uncomfortable bending. A drawer below stores baking pans. The microwave oven is also at a convenient height. Cabinets: Wilsonart. Door hardware: Hettich America. Floor: Florida Tile.

CENTER ISLAND

Right: Solid surfacing counters are customized with inset strips of faux metal laminate set on a matching mottled base. The shape of the island is in direct contrast with the nearest countertops—if the two were pushed together, there would be a perfect fit! Solid surfacing and laminate: Wilsonart. Appliances: General Electric.

A PLAYFUL MIX

If bright colors are your cup of tea, why not have some fun with them in your kitchen? A variety of colors, patterns, and textures gives this kitchen a look it can call its very own.

Cabinets in four distinct colors are free from traditional decorations. Shiny knobs match the room's appliances. The professional-looking equipment is surrounded by cabinets for a built-in look. But where some contemporary kitchens use cabinet fronts on the appliances to make them blend in, this design refuses to conceal the stainless fronts.

Vinyl flooring combines a section of checkerboard to coordinate with the cabinets, a darker speckled variation of the counters, and a light irregular walkway.

FLOOR ART

Right: Three different vinyl patterns create a walkway that extends from the breakfast room to the kitchen door. The professional-style range gives the festive decor a more serious side. Stove and oven: Thermador. Floor: Kentile.

SURFACE APPEAL

Left: Frameless cabinets in three colors create interesting blocks around the commercial-looking appliances. The granite countertop and backsplash are a neutral and elegant addition. Designer: John Everage and Krista Everage. Styling: Donna Pizzi. Cabinets: Gary Hartmark, Hartmark Finewood Designs.

MODERN STORAGE

Tall cabinets are an essential part of this kitchen's contemporary, built-in appeal. The cabinetry steps lightly around side-by-side undermount sinks, each with its own faucet. Designer: Jackie Naylor Interiors.

TOTAL LIVING SPACE

Limited space was the challenge in this kitchen. It had to be carefully planned to satisfy everyday needs as well as those that arise when entertaining.

A small rounded peninsula creates a spot for light dining and doubles as a buffer to the adjoining family room. A self-serve bar area, complete with undermount sink, refrigerator, and freezer, finds its niche near the built-in entertainment center.

Sleek cabinets, without hardware, turn the design into a contemporary dream. High-gloss black on the counters, backsplash, and chairs enhances the light cabinets. To maximize the space, the designer extended wall cabinets all the way to the ceiling and added a center island. Less frequently used items can be stored near the ceiling, while everyday dishes remain within easy reach.

THE ENTERTAINER

With a small sink, refrigerator, and freezer, the wet bar is ready for guests. Built-in shelves for a television and stereo equipment copy the kitchen's color scheme.

FILLED WITH PERSONALITY

There's more to a kitchen than cabinets, appliances, and countertops. Many people spend a great deal of time in their kitchens, yet often they keep personal touches to a minimum. Collections are put in dining and living rooms, while interesting bowls and pitchers are stored behind closed doors.

This sunny kitchen uses open shelves and glass-front cabinets to put colorful pieces out in the open. Neat rows of contemporary light fixtures hang above the island. The island's arched-back seating adds even more personality.

An unusual feature is that two separate sinks are located next to each other, each with its own pull-out spray and soap dispenser. The large windows mimic the design. Natural stone counters give the kitchen an elegant appeal that flows into adjoining living space.

TWO SINKS

Side-by-side windows do more than let in extra light. They're a mirror image of the double sink set-up directly below them. The island's curving design adds a shapely element to the airy kitchen. Designer: Ken Neumann. Cooktop: Dacor.

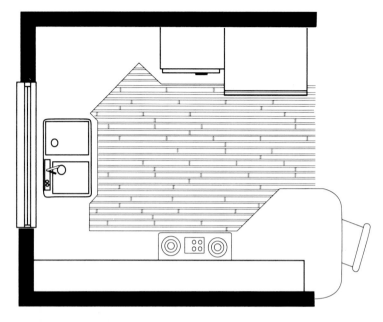

SPACE-SAVING SOLUTIONS

There's no reason why a small kitchen can't be as functional and attractive as a larger one. Storage may be less plentiful. Counters won't run endlessly with open work space. But careful planning can assure that the work triangle and overall design meet the owners' needs.

To brighten up a small kitchen, use light colors like those shown here. If you like wood, select a lighter or natural finish. If rich, dark woods are your preference, lighten up the other surfaces. Adding personal touches, such as artwork or an angled floor plan, takes the focus off the room's size. The angel sconce in the kitchen on the right is an original created by the designer.

An island or peninsula can add an interesting shape, cabinets, and workspace to almost any kitchen. Informal seating is an added bonus in kitchens, like those shown here, that cannot comfortably accommodate a table.

ANGLED LAYOUT

Left: By angling the dishwasher, the designer of this small kitchen created the illusion of more space and added interest to the plan. An extended countertop on the opposite side of the room becomes a breakfast bar for two. Designer: Kathy A. Maraglio, CKD/NKBA Design Competition 1994.

CITY LOFT

This kitchen might be limited in size, but it's big on style. Items such as the 1950s bar stools, marble-topped table, and Andy Warhol painting combine to make the design an aesthetic treat. Designer: Alvin Schneider. Light fixture: Lighting Center.

HIGH-TECH GOOD LOOKS

There's no mistaken identity in this kitchen. From its striking color scheme and staggered cabinets to the floating light fixtures, the design is purely contemporary. Stainless appliances and door hardware add a professional spin.

A kitchen as utterly contemporary as this one might seem sterile to some. But friendly details, including open shelving for cookbooks and a customized space for a unique collection of miniature houses, take some of the hard edge off the design. The multi-tiered and multifunctional island also has a softer side, providing casual dining for two.

FOR THE COOK

Above: A shiny cooktop and range hood combination is matched by the open racks below. The room's silver, white, and blue scheme gets high marks for style. Range: Thermador. Hood: Best SPA.

CENTER ISLAND

Left: Offering an informal dining area, open counters for preparing meals, and extra storage, this island plays a big role in the kitchen. Open displays add personal touches to the sleek design.

EXTRA STORAGE

Right: Sleek cabinets step around the main sink, adding interest and plenty of storage. Take note of the wine bottles tucked neatly away in the island base. Designers: Deborah Litz-Beard and Gary Hancock. Cabinet hardware: Siro Designs, Inc.

STREAMLINE IN WHITE

Everyone loves a bright, sunny kitchen. But if you're short on windows, look to this kitchen for bright ideas. Simple pendants hang from the ceiling and provide general illumination. Plenty of undercabinet lighting ensures sufficient task lighting for working at the counters. The bright white decor and light wood floor help keep the look light and airy. The sleek, built-in cabinets, free from hardware, are the heart of the streamlined, contemporary design.

In addition to a lack of windows, this space had a very obvious structural limitation in the form of a large pillar. But instead of hiding the pillar, the designer made the most of it, making it the center of an informal dining space. This kitchen is a perfect example of how a great design can turn structural difficulties into assets.

BUILT-INS

White wall ovens and the refrigerator dressed with a cabinet front blend into this handsome kitchen. The adjacent desk offers a functional spot for paperwork. Designer: Joan Halperin Interior Design.

SMALL SPACE

Above: A gleaming design and clever plan make the most of the kitchen's limited space. Continuous runs of cabinets provide ample storage.

DINING IN

Left: Informal meals can be enjoyed by three at the pedestal-style table built around a structural support.

HIGH STYLE FROM ITALY

Contemporary designs share sleek lines and bold styling. Whether the cabinets are finished wood or glossy laminate, they're almost always frameless. The two kitchens showcased here have Italian cabinetry as a focal point. Both use basic black and a trendy shade of blue as accents.

Interesting curves are almost playful in the kitchen on the right. The arches are echoed in the door hardware and wall cabinets above the sink. This convex and concave arrangement is unusual, but doesn't interfere with the room's work and walk aisle.

The kitchen on the left, like many modern-design spaces, features basic shapes and straight lines. Wall cabinets resemble trimmed boxes set upon display shelves. Marblesque base cabinets feature small round knobs.

IN CONTRAST

Left: A mix of shapes and finishes gives this kitchen its raw good looks. A small shelf puts an open backsplash to work. Designer: Gae Aulenti. Cabinets: Snaidero.

SHAPELY LAYOUT

Right: Semicircles add interest to this built-in kitchen. Black and teal are used for dramatic accents. Designer: Pininfarina. Cabinets: Snaidero.

LIGHTENING UP A PRACTICAL DESIGN

If entertaining and cooking are two of your favorite activities, you need a well-planned kitchen. Plenty of work space, storage, and modern appliances are necessities. And then, why not lighten up your hardworking kitchen with a touch of fun?

The rotating pot rack and teak-topped center island provide a focal point and give this kitchen much of its personality. The island is simple and elegant. Its wood countertop makes a large, attractive work space and provides casual dining space for two. The light gray laminate cabinets, dressed up with a darker stripe, add decorative flair to the generous storage space.

The amateur chef will fall in love with this kitchen's stainless steel range, three separate sinks, and ample storage and work spaces. The decorating enthusiast will appreciate the attractive design elements. There's something for everyone in this contemporary kitchen!

CUSTOM POT RACK

Left: Pots and pans suspended from a cedar ceiling reflect the homeowners' love of cooking. The overall look of the kitchen is crisp, clean, and modern. Designer: Trudy McGinnis, CKD. Pot rack: John Medwedeff/21st Century Forge. Range: Viking. Floor: Ipocork.

CENTER ISLAND

Below: Teak and laminate team up in this spacious center island. The kitchen boasts three sinks: the one shown here for food preparation, another for clean-up, and the third, located at the bar, for washing glasses. Faucets: Grohe. Cabinets: Crystal Cabinets.

DOUBLE IMAGE WITHOUT MIRRORS

Below: Space for informal dining is provided at a lowered counter on the back side of the cooking island. Tamboured base panels match the cabinets. Designers: Diana Valentine, CKD, & Brit Goldstine/NKBA Design Competition 1993. Cabinets: Fieldstone. Range: Thermador. Countertop: DuPont Corian.

Even in small kitchens, radius cabinets have a way of opening up spaces. Edges become less severe and create more comfortable walkways. In this kitchen, flowing curves are repeated in mirror-like fashion to create a symmetrical layout.

The semicircular center island repeats the kitchen's curved design. If the island were pushed forward to meet the main run of counterspace, it would be a near perfect fit. The island top holds a four-burner cooktop. On the back, a breakfast bar is lowered to seat two or three comfortably.

The kitchen features a mix of materials—marble, tile, wood, and solid surfacing—that promotes the bright, contemporary feel. Antique white cabinets feature a bold frameless construction; the neutral finish promotes a more inviting feeling than the stark white that's often found in contemporary kitchens. Custom panels on the appliances have a built-in appearance, contributing to the kitchen's modern style. Down to the vertical door handles, the look is up-to-date.

Right: Curved cabinet arrangements create a spacious walkway through the kitchen. The sink window, skylight, and recessed lighting team with the light color scheme for a bright and airy design. Dishwasher: Asko/Asea. Sink and fittings: DuPont Corian. Windows: Weathervane.

EXCITING FINISHES

There's a lot more to selecting countertops and cabinets than deciding upon the material and style. There are no limits when it comes to colors and finishes, especially in contemporary kitchens, where nearly anything goes. What a big manufacturer doesn't offer, a talented craftsman will figure out a way to create.

This trio of kitchens glows with shiny surfaces. And although the three look very different, they're all prime examples of contemporary design. Professional-style appliances—common in contemporary kitchens—appeal to the gourmet cook and add a decorative touch with their matter-of-fact styling. Cabinets, like those shown here, usually feature flat door panels with interesting finishes.

SHAPELY PLAN

Above: Convex and concave cabinet arrangements are an interesting contrast to the straightforward design. The bold color scheme is highlighted by black counters and a rich wood floor. Designer: Pininfarina. Cabinets: Snaidero.

GOURMET COOKING

Right: Brass trim accents the magnificent range hood above the restaurant-style cooktop, which offers six burners and a barbecue. Designer: Cheryl Casey Ross. Cooktop and hood: Russell Range.

COOL DRAWERS

Above: With its shiny surfaces and hardworking appliances, this kitchen embodies high-tech. Pull-out refrigerator drawers blend in with the cabinets and put food close to the prep areas.
Designer: Harry Haynes, CKD. Refrigerators: Sub-Zero.

EYE ON THE ENVIRONMENT

The greening of society has prompted homeowners and designers to think environmentally. As a result, kitchens are becoming more earth-friendly and energy efficient. The designer of this maple kitchen made a point of choosing appliances with lower energy-use ratings.

The designer also borrowed the earthy color scheme from Mother Nature. Large windows take advantage of sunlight to illuminate and warm the space. Ebony accents on the frameless cabinets, stainless steel appliance panels, and suspended low-voltage lights give the kitchen a contemporary look. Although stainless can be cold, it looks less sterile when surrounded by this kitchen's granite countertops and washed wood cabinets. The tone is further mellowed by the natural finish on the cabinets and the butcher-block work area.

Rather than waste open floor space, the kitchen's designer planned a small center island for the gas cooktop. A granite-topped breakfast bar runs alongside, creating a spot for quick snacks. This wonderfully earth-friendly kitchen is user-friendly, too!

EXTRA STORAGE

Above: The focal point of this maple kitchen is the center wall cabinet with ebony trim and molding. It seems to float between the two large windows. Cabinets: Brookhaven. Trim and moldings: Wood-Mode.

FOOD PREP AREA

Left: Part of the main countertop is dropped and covered with butcher block. The result is a comfortable workspace for the cook. Designer: Janice Stone Thomas, ASID, CKD/Stonewood Cabinetry & Design.

WORK TRIANGLE

The cooktop is easily accessible from the refrigerator and sink. Stainless steel panels and a single countertop give the appliances a high-tech look.
Appliances: Jenn-Air.

WARMED WITH PATCHWORK

Soft contemporary kitchens usually lighten up their sleek surfaces and layouts with some traditional decoration. You might not expect a patchwork quilt design to find a home amidst black solid surfacing counters and glossy faux maple cabinets. But here, a patchwork of mosaic squares meets up with a contemporary design to create a warm, relaxed, modern space.

The tile blanket is enhanced by colorful ceramics displayed in glass-front cabinets and cushions on the island chairs. An inlaid white dotted line in the black counters is another custom touch.

This kitchen was designed to invite guests in, but keep them out of the cook's way. The two large peninsulas serve this function: The extended countertops not only add work space, they also work as room dividers. Both hosts and guests can be comfortable as meals are prepared in this appealing space.

OPEN DISPLAYS

Left: Often contemporary kitchens feature continuous runs of closed cabinets. Here, open shelves and see-through doors let some of the home-owners' colorful ceramics soften the decor. Cabinets: Heritage Custom Kitchens. Countertop and sink: DuPont Corian. Faucet: Grohe.

WORK TRIANGLE

Right: The L-shape peninsula works overtime by separating guests from the cook's primary workspace. The sink, cooktop, and refrigerator are all within a few steps of each other. Designers: Wendi Wilkins and Judy McCaffrey/NKBA Design Competition 1994. Cooktop: Thermador. Hood: Vent-A-Hood. Tile: Dal Tile.

OPEN TO TRADITION

If you're planning a contemporary kitchen, don't throw away that classic dining room set—make it part of your design. Your cherished old pieces can work beautifully in a soft contemporary setting.

In the contemporary cooking area, floor-to-ceiling cabinets provide plenty of storage, topped with spaces for wine bottles. The center island also packs in lots of storage, plus the primary sink and cooktop. Second and third sinks, in separate expanses of butcher block, are ideal when two people are working in the kitchen.

The hardwood floor smooths the transition to the more traditional dining area. The molded hutch and dinette set are country at heart, but they fit right in with the rest of the soft contemporary kitchen.

EAT-IN DESIGN

Above: Carved woods and glowing sunlight soften the contemporary kitchen, while adding a more formal dining space within it. The area is set apart by the tile floor and traditional furniture.

TWO COOKS

Right: At least two people can work comfortably at this spacious island. Three sinks and butcher block create a trio of food prep areas. The cooktop is a multiple panel arrangement. Cooktop: Jenn-Air. Refrigerator: Sub-Zero. Wall ovens: KitchenAid.

EXTRA STORAGE

Horizontal handles add both convenience and decoration to the numerous kitchen cabinets. Two walls of built-ins keep the up-to-date decor free from clutter.
Designer: John J. Quinn II.

A TOUCH OF CLASS

White kitchens are perhaps the most neutral of all. They can be contemporary or traditional, country or Californian. It's the accessories that truly give them their flavor. With its white countertops speckled with blue diamonds and coordinating tile backsplash and floor, this white kitchen is soft contemporary.

The galley layout is wide open, flowing into a sunny breakfast room at one end. Plentiful cabinets keep dishes and cooking utensils out of view; storage is essential to the room's clean, uncluttered look. The up-to-date space is softened by floral and striped wallcoverings. This kitchen is also convertible: If the homeowners want to give the space a new look inexpensively, they can update the wallcovering and borders.

BUILT-IN OVEN

Above right: This recessed oven blends with the surrounding raised-panel cabinets. The adjacent countertop offers a safe landing spot for casseroles and baking dishes hot from the oven. Appliances: Maytag.

BAR SINK

Right: A second sink works overtime when guests are visiting or extra hands are needed to rinse vegetables. Designer: Kitchens by Krengel. Countertop: Wilsonart.

FAMILY SPACE

Left: With a built-in desk, roomy walkway, and adjoining breakfast room, this layout is designed for a family to comfortably mix and mingle beyond mealtimes. Ceramic tile: American Olean.

HIGH ON DRAMA

A number of interesting elements in this kitchen add up to one dramatic design. The cabinets take their look from the shoji screens that fill the kitchen and the adjoining room. With frosted glass fronts, the cabinets mimic the finely crafted screens. The drama is heightened by an open-beam ceiling.

Forgoing stark and bright whites, this contemporary design is replete with softer and richer tones. The natural stone counter has black veining that conceals the outer edges of the neo-angle sink and gas cooktop. Arched door hardware is interesting, yet simple. The floor is a variety of neutral shades blending together. The overall effect is to combine drama and simplicity for an unforgettable look.

MODERN DECOR

Below: Contemporary accents in this kitchen include black hardware and a rugged countertop. The mirrored backsplash creates the illusion of more space. Natural wood cabinets are softened with faux screens.

DINING AREA

Right: Mood lighting streaming down from the vaulted ceiling delicately illuminates an adjacent dining room. Shoji screens double as room dividers and decoration.
Designer: Sheron Bailey, CKD. Interior designer: John J. Schneider, CID. Lighting designer: Linda Ferry. Architect: William David Martin, AIA.

CLEAN-CUT LINES AND SURFACES

Contemporary designs can work just as nicely for everyday family life and entertaining as their country cousins do. In fact, what a kitchen looks like has nothing to do with its functionality. This practical layout creates a total living environment where friends and family can mix and mingle without feeling cramped.

Light and dark surfaces play up this kitchen's contemporary design, but natural sunlight and tinted cabinets soften the decor. The impressive island offers a second sink and extra storage, including spaces for wine bottles. The outer curve of the island is for casual dining. It's also an ideal conversation place—out of the kitchen's main work triangle. A separate table can accommodate more formal dining conveniently close to the cooking area.

BUILT-IN TV

Above left: A small entertainment system rises from inside the island for viewing pleasure. When the TV is pushed down, a circular top blends with surrounding counters. Designer: Janie Jordan, CKD, IIDA.

HIDEAWAYS

Left: Counters are kept clutter-free with the help of tambour doors that hide kitchen essentials. Black appliances stand out among the tinted custom cabinets.

EAT-IN PLAN

Right: The breakfast bar and dining area each serve a purpose in this active kitchen. The space is kept bright with free-flowing sunlight and dramatic track lighting.

An extended island becomes an informal dining area with the addition of well-cushioned metal chairs. Professional-style appliances shine with stainless surfaces. Refrigerator: Sub-Zero. Sink: Franke.

SOFTENED WITH PINE

Who says a contemporary kitchen can't have traditional cabinetry? If you like contemporary kitchens, but the rest of your home is decorated in a country style, a design like this one might fit right in.

A pleasant hint of country, abundant natural pine cabinets fill the walls. The cabinetry contrasts with contemporary traits such as high-gloss black countertops, bold fabrics and wallcoverings, and sleek stainless appliances. Glass-front cabinets, another country touch, allow the owners to display their china collection. The unusual window treatment nearby provides yet another contemporary contrast.

If you're torn between two different styles, use this kitchen for inspiration and as a reminder that you *can* have it both ways.

BUILT-IN DESK

Above right: Open storage above a floating counter creates a desk for skimming through a cookbook or answering the phone. Bright fabrics and wallcoverings complement the natural wood tones. Designer: Lisa McCauley.

CENTER ISLAND

Right: The recessed panel cabinets and open storage are country kitchen touches. Topped by dark granite counters and accompanied by teal and peach fabrics and wallcoverings, they're also a natural fit in this contemporary plan.

FILLED WITH CHARM

R ich hardwood flooring and a bold shade of blue give this design its elegant appeal. The white kitchen features traditional detailing, including inset panel doors and gallery molding on the cabinets.

Classic touches are plentiful. Matching decorative tiles are used on the countertops and backsplash for continuity. An arched window lets natural light illuminate the triple-bowl sink and integral three-part cooktop. Black appliances stand out among the white cabinets for a crisp contrast. Traditional details such as the ornate supports under the island countertop, balloon window treatment, and overhead ceiling fan add the finishing touches.

BUILT-IN DESK

Right: **There's room to pull up a chair at the custom desk. Glass-front cabinets above the desk show off colorful ceramic ware.** *Tile: American Olean. Dishwasher: KitchenAid.*

SINK AREA

Above: **The extra-large sink is divided for added convenience. Pretty fabric dresses up the window and lets the sun shine in.** *Designer: Mimi W. Smith. Architect: Charles Roberts Drafting Co. Sink: Kohler. Range: Jenn-Air.*

EATING IN

Right: **Classic hardware and floor-to-ceiling windows are opulent additions to this eat-in kitchen. The extended island counter puts food and drink within easy reach of the table.**

A FLORAL FLOURISH

A traditional white kitchen is versatile enough to adapt to a variety of looks. If you choose the basics for the counters and cabinets, you'll find it easy to update the look in future years. Some fresh paint and wallcoverings, and even new flooring and door hardware, can dramatically change the decor.

Here, painted tile murals and pastel fabrics add a springlike, feminine note to the basic white kitchen. The eat-in design is dressed up with florals on the walls and ceiling. The floral theme is echoed in the painted tiles on the island and backsplash. Ornate valances and woodworking add the finishing touches.

This charming space is also a super-practical family kitchen. An island puts the cooktop at the center of the room and supplies sufficient counterspace. A built-in desk is ideal for leaving messages or planning meals. Guests can help themselves at a pretty wet bar. There's even a spot for solo meals near the full dining set. Even in December, family members and guests can enjoy dining in a garden of flowers.

BREAKFAST ROOM

Left: An open layout makes room for an everyday eating area. From the billowy window treatments and floral wall-coverings to the chandelier, the decor is light, floral, and airy. *Wallpaper and fabric: The Twigs. Ruffle: Brunschwig & Fils.*

MINIBAR

Right: With a hand-painted wildlife backdrop, this wet bar sports traditional accents, including detailed lattice-work used for the wine rack. It's an ideal set-up for enter-taining. *Designer: Susie Leader Interiors, Inc. Tile murals: Debbie Seymour.*

BUILT-IN DESK

Above: Custom cabinets work just as nicely over this desk as they do in the rest of the kitchen. Interior lighting and classic molding lend a formal look. *Cabinets: Mike Lange, Sterling Woods.*

SPECKLED WITH SUNLIGHT

The colors may be soft, but this kitchen's design is hard-working. Extensive runs of countertops, extra cabinetry, and a full range of appliances make this a great space for the dedicated cook. The professional-style range is an added delight for the weekend gourmet.

The traditional decor is achieved with lightly painted cabinets and earth-tone tiles. The open soffits are backed with a row of windows that visually expand the space. Clear glass cabinets let sunlight flow freely into the kitchen and adjoining family room. A painted bouquet on the backing tile livens up the muted colors with a perennial reminder of sunny spring.

COOKING CENTER

Below: The cook won't lack for oven space with these two wall ovens, topped with a built-in microwave/convection oven. Pull-out drawers keep canned foods and other staples handy. Designer: Bonnie Sachs, ASID. Double oven: Gaggenau USA. Microwave oven: Creda.

MINI GREENHOUSE

Above: An extended ledge and greenhouse window are ideal for indoor plants. The painted shade complements the kitchen's floral throw rug. Shade: Studio Shades. Sink: Kohler. Faucet: Grohe America.

GOURMET TOUCHES

Right: Colorful tiles, including a decorative mural, soften the grill's commercial-style look. A functional warming drawer is an added bonus amidst the traditional cabinetry. Grill: Gaggenau USA. Tile: Ann Sacks Tile & Stone. Countertop: DuPont Corian. Cooktop: Russell Range. Warming oven: Thermador.

EATING IN

Below: A double sink is conveniently located near the dining area for mealtime clean-up. To the sink's left, a tambour cabinet keeps small appliances off the counters and out of view. Designers: Candace Ihlenfeldt and Brit Goldstine/NKBA Design Competition 1993. Cabinets: Fieldstone.

RICH IN AMBIENCE

There are many ways to visually open up a kitchen. This one uses rich wood tones and clean, uncluttered lines. Notice how a natural finish highlights the cabinets' cherry grain to make them a focal point. Simple black hardware adds subtle decoration to the cabinetry, while light solid surfacing seems to extend the countertops.

The design is filled with user-friendly features. Counterspace below the microwave and adjacent to the wall ovens provides a landing space for hot dishes. Tambour doors discreetly hide away small appliances. Marble on the island and backsplash is as appealing as it is functional. The abundant cabinets are rescued from monotony by occasional open shelves.

In the adjoining eating area, a wall of windows lets the sunshine in. Oak flooring is used in both areas for continuity, unifying the space and contributing to the warm ambience of both rooms.

KITCHEN HELP

Right: The double oven, microwave oven, bar sink, and countertops all come in handy when more than one person is working in the kitchen. Cooktop and oven: Dacor. Microwave oven: GE. Refrigerator: Sub-Zero.

A BREATH OF FRESH AIR

A kitchen doesn't have to be flashy or flamboyant to make a statement. Sometimes the simplest designs have the strongest impact. Here, all the pieces fit together beautifully in an outstanding design.

The light cabinets and countertops give a refreshing, airy feeling. Bold tile diamonds are used sparingly, lending just the right amount of interest to the floors and back-splash. A small peninsula offers seating and enough counterspace for one person to enjoy a quick breakfast and the morning paper. More traditional features are the square raised panels and small knobs on the cabinets.

With its perfect balance of traditional styling and touches of red, this is a simple design that makes a lasting impression.

BREAKFAST BAR

Left: This small peninsula provides comfortable seating for one and doubles as a partial room divider. Fancy glassware has a home in glass-front cabinets. Design: Mark Combs.

HOT SPOT

Right: A separate oven and cooktop are well ventilated by the handsome range hood. The double band of tile adds color without being overbearing.

MADE FOR ENTERTAINING

Once upon a time, guests didn't spend much time in their hosts' kitchen. But times have changed. Today's plans are designed with many considerations, including entertaining, in mind. Larger spaces offer sit-down islands where guests can converse with the cook. It's not unusual to see a dinette or even a comfy sofa in the kitchen or an adjacent great room.

With all its interesting shapes, this layout is designed so that more than two people can work in the kitchen at the same time, while enjoying the company of their guests. The cabinets are traditional, and their placement is elegant. Black counters are a stunning contrast. On one side of the kitchen, a handy butcher-block table provides cutting space. On the other side, a fully appointed cooking center includes a double wall oven, microwave oven, cooktop, and wine storage.

DINING TABLE

Above: Who says an eat-in kitchen can't be elegant? A striking open-beam design, large windows, and wood table create a formal dining area right near the hub of kitchen activity.

FOOD PREP

Right: Plenty of counterspace surrounds the sink. A unique undercabinet bookshelf can hold cookbooks or leather-bound classics. Designer: Beth Mellina.

EXTRA STORAGE

A creative plan uses traditional cabinets to maximize storage capacity. A mix of sizes, shapes, and styles lends visual interest.

AROUND AN OCTAGON

If you like classic architecture, but often select contemporary furniture and accessories, don't despair. Combine the two looks in your kitchen—there's nothing wrong with blending old and new. This kitchen demonstrates just how good classic architectural features can look in an up-to-date setting.

The traditional design works around a large octagonal island stepped up for privacy and additional storage. Corner cabinets mimic the shapely island, as does the overhead lighting set-up. A diagonal hardwood floor and more angled cabinets create a graceful entry into the adjoining family space. The two areas flow together, yet remain separate.

Although the kitchen is filled with traditional elements, such as the pillars, molding, and arched doorways, the look is crisp and up-to-date. Among some more contemporary features are the built-in appliances and staggered wall cabinets. The result of the style blending is a real contemporary classic.

GREAT ROOM

Below: An impressive hardwood floor leads the way from the kitchen to the family room. Pillars, angled cabinets, and a creatively placed island keep the two rooms separate. Designer: Jane Burdette Manko/NKBA Design Competition 1993. Cabinets: Quaker Maid.

CENTER ISLAND

Right: A cooktop on the octagonal island is conveniently located near the sink and refrigerator. The stepped-up island offers extra storage and acts as a divider from the adjoining family room. Sink and countertop: DuPont Corian. Dishwasher: In-Sink-Erator. Cooktop: Thermador. Refrigerator: Sub-Zero.

Above: Surrounding counter-space and accessibility from two sides make this sink ideal for food preparation.

STEPS TO SATISFACTION

We're so accustomed to seeing countertops run straight and on an even plane that when they don't, we do a double take. This interesting kitchen is definitely worth a second look. The jagged countertop, which creates comfortable nooks for working at the sink and sitting at the island, grabs the spotlight. Look a little longer, though, and you'll notice all the amenities packed into the layout.

There's a stacked washer and dryer, separate food prep sink, and an elevated dishwasher to save stooping and crouching. The tiered island design adds an element of privacy and plenty of interest. The light cabinets and green island counter give this unusual design its traditional feel.

HIDDEN FEATURES

Left: The dishwasher is raised to eliminate the need for bending when loading dishes. The landing space in front of the microwave oven is practical and safe. An open counter above the oven is perfect for hot dishes. Designer: Kitchens By Krengel. Stylist: Nancy Wall Hopkins.

MULTI-USE ISLAND

Right: This island's unusual shape is stunning to look at, but its many practical attributes make it truly outstanding. A table, storage, oven, and second sink are all built in. Cabinets: Design Line Cabinets.

RIGHT AT HOME

Combining a kitchen, family room, and dining area into one spacious layout (often called a Great Room) has a lot of advantages. Not only do you gain footage for kitchen necessities such as storage, you also create a multipurpose room for family and friends to enjoy. The ideal Great Room set-up features an open plan that allows each space to remain independent.

This traditional kitchen is laid out so that the cook can look out into the family room and chat with family or friends. White molding, a hardwood floor, and a neutral green painted wall tie the whole room together.

In the kitchen area, the white cabinets and counters show finely crafted traditional styling. The wood dinette is placed in front of large glass windows which, along with the chandelier, make the space a little dressier. Traffic flows easily from one part of the Great Room into the others, making it a perfect space for family dinners and casual entertaining.

BAR SERVICE

Above: This complete bar lets guests help themselves without setting foot in the main kitchen area.

DOUBLE CHILL

Right: How many times have you wished for more refrigerator space? A separate refrigerator and freezer offer more than enough room for everyday and entertainment needs.

GREAT ROOM

Left: An adjoining family room shares the kitchen's classic charm. The cooking center is arranged so the cook can socialize with family and friends. Designer: Mike Boyette Kitchens & Baths. Cooktop: Dacor. Countertop: Avonite.

ANGLED FOR SUCCESS

Angles not only add interest to a design; they can also allow you to take advantage of unused space. In this kitchen, the angled island creates an open path for work and traffic flow. It's also multifunctional.

The kitchen layout actually includes two distinct work areas—one for every day and one for special occasions. The main kitchen is an L-shape plan that includes a solid surfacing countertop, double oven, cooktop, and sink. A massive palladian window fits right in with the light traditional decor. The large-capacity refrigerator stands between the primary kitchen and an area designed especially for caterers, with storage, a sink, and a dishwasher.

The marble-topped island offers room for casual dining. With a second sink and dishwasher, it's ideal for entertaining. Whether it's being used for quiet family dinners or large parties, this kitchen really performs.

DUAL USE

Left: The main part of the kitchen opens into an open space with a second sink and dishwasher that are used when the homeowners entertain. *Lighting: Halo. Refrigerator: Sub-Zero. Second sink: Kohler. Refrigerator: Sub-Zero.*

CLASSIC LOOKS

Right: The entire kitchen area is pulled together with a richly stained hardwood floor and soaring ceilings. The full-overlay white cabinets are detailed with crown molding. *Designers: Patti Lawson, CKD, and Michael Pachan/NKBA Design Competition 1993. Cabinets: Quality Custom. Ovens and dishwashers: KitchenAid. Main sink and counters: DuPont Corian. Cooktop: Jenn-Air.*

Above: *Staggered cabinet heights add interest to this roomy family kitchen. The arched configurations mimic the raised ceiling. A striking geometric design in the resilient floor emphasizes the island.* Designers: John A. Buscarello, ASID, and George Magyar, CKD. Stylist: Pamela Abrahams.

Above: *Even the youngest family members can help with food preparation and baking. The pull-out step stool makes the sink easier for kids to use.* Cabinets: Bertch Cabinet Co.

Left: *A microwave oven is neatly tucked into island base cabinets. This puts the appliance at a child-friendly height and takes it off the countertop.* Appliances: KitchenAid. Floor: Armstrong.

THE FAMILY PLAN

If you have kids, you know how much use a kitchen can see on an average day and how much time you and your family spend there. A truly well-planned family kitchen is user-friendly for even your youngest child. It allows all family members to participate in preparing meals, as well as eating them. It should also be comfortable and pleasing to the eye.

This kitchen was designed with a family in mind. Numerous special features enable little hands to help out with kitchen work. In the looks department, black dashes routed into solid surfacing countertops grab the spotlight. Arched wood and moldings that mimic the raised ceiling are another focal point. Practical as well as attractive, this kitchen will be used and enjoyed by all family members.

EDGE TREATMENT

Above: A decorative countertop edge is a great place to show some creativity. This line of black dashes adds interest to the entire room. Solid surfacing: Wilsonart. Tile: Florida Tile. Faucet: Delta.

BREAKFAST ROOM

Left: For families, an eat-in kitchen is almost as much a necessity as it is a luxury. This space is illuminated by natural light.

DRESSED IN WHITE

If there's one trend in kitchen design that's come to the forefront in recent years, it's the lightening of cabinet colors and finishes. White has become one of the top color choices and seems to be here to stay. Already spacious, this kitchen seems even bigger and brighter with its white cabinets.

Traditional details are found in the range hood, raised panel doors, and molding. The octagonal island stands out with a rich speckled top. In addition to providing ample work and buffet space, the island ties the plan together. Without it, the wood floor might seem like an endless run from the refrigerator to the primary sink. The kitchen is packed with modern conveniences, including a double wall oven and second sink.

CENTER ISLAND

Left: A kitchen of this scope has ample storage and counter space, but the island offers a centralized work area. Elegance is added with a polished hardwood floor, accented by an inlaid border stripe and lovely floral arrangement painted behind the cooktop.

EATING IN

Right: Built-in benches help create this dining nook, complete with faux foliage chandelier, in a quiet corner of the kitchen. Designer: Beth Gillin.

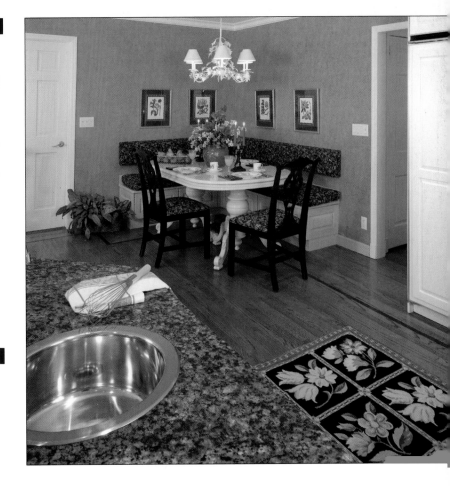

OPEN-ENDED DESIGN FLOW

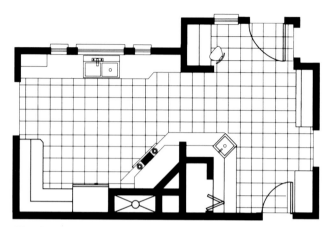

This floor plan shows how the space flows from pantry to kitchen. The dining room is not included because it was not changed in the remodeling.

Sometimes the most appealing kitchens are those that turn a "problem" into an advantage. When it was time to remodel this space, the designer couldn't remove existing walls to make one large area. So the plan remains divided into three parts: kitchen, butler's pantry, and dining room.

Original doors leading from the kitchen to the other rooms were widened. The once challenging entryways now lend interesting architectural elements, while separating the spaces by function. The butler's pantry was also updated to blend with the new light and airy kitchen.

A Palladian window lets natural light cascade into the kitchen, which is further brightened by white cabinets and granite counters. The magnificent tile mural behind the cooktop reflects the homeowners' interest in art. An elegant pastel floor runs from the dining room all the way to the butler's pantry, visually uniting the entire space.

BUTLER'S PANTRY

Left: The new and improved butler's pantry includes a sink and a built-in desk that's tucked away for privacy. Oversized arched doorways allow the pantry, kitchen, and dining room to flow into each other. Designer: Dagmar Theil, CKD/NKBA Design Competition 1994. Sink: Kohler. Faucets: Franke.

DECORATIVE NOOK

With an eye-catching Spanish tile mural behind it, the gas cooktop becomes the focal point of the white kitchen. *Cabinets: Cotton Wood. Cooktop: Thermador. Sink: Blanco. Faucet: Franke.*

PLAYING ALL THE ANGLES

Angled floor plans have a number of advantages in kitchen design. They add visual interest to straight runs of cabinets and to the kitchen in general. They can also help maximize space, especially when there isn't a lot of extra square footage to work with. In recent designs, you'll often find a cooktop or sink placed in an angled corner.

In this traditional kitchen, it's the cooktop that occupies a corner. The center island mimics the angled shape to create an open walkway between the cooktop and primary sink. Another interesting angled nook contains a wet bar, complete with a second sink. Angles are the key to a design that combines great looks with space-saving practicality.

CABINET PLAN

Left: Cabinets are stained a rich traditional color, but their layout is rather nontraditional. Staggering the lengths and depths of wall cabinets adds visual interest to this formal kitchen.
Designer: Robert Duffield.
Cabinets: Crestwood.

WET BAR

Right: The wet bar is angled to face guests entering the kitchen. The sink can be used during meal preparation as a secondary work area.

IN PLEASANT COMPANY

Below: An angled design gives storage in the dining area its own identity. Open shelves and vertical wine storage lend interest to the traditional room. Burgundy trim and molding top off all the cabinets. Designer: Rita Foulk.

This kitchen may not be oversized, but it's so well planned that a lot of amenities fit in. The flowing layout, complete with bi-level center island, offers plenty of storage and built-in features. The traditional raised-panel doors start off the room's appealing decor. It's accented with speckled countertops and dressy gold door hardware.

The primary work center is located in an L-shape layout. Behind the island, a wall of cabinets creates room for more kitchen necessities to be stored out of view. In the kitchen's dining area, the cabinets line the wall, forming smoothly flowing curves where they meet the corner of the room. Light colors, traditional styling, and a large window over the sink make this kitchen a pleasant, sunny, relaxing space.

Right: The major components of this sunny kitchen are arranged in an L-shape layout. The arched window and two-tiered island are as convenient as they are pleasing to look at.

BE OUR GUEST

Some kitchens are so charming they seem to wordlessly invite you in. This trio blends welcoming surroundings with practical layouts for wonderful results. Each kitchen is filled with great ideas to consider in your own home.

Adding a separate table and chairs or island seating creates a convenient eat-in design. Fabrics always add a soft touch to kitchens. If you have a shapely new window, though, you might want to skip the billowy treatments and let the window's shape be seen inside and outside the house.

It's always fun to add some interest to the walls and back-splash. Paint them a favorite color, choose contrasting tiles, or bring in a patterned wallcovering. Other comforts, such as a built-in television or window seat, turn the kitchen into a relaxed living area. All these suggestions have been implemented in the kitchens shown here—take a look and decide which ones might work for you!

TASTE OF HONEY

Above: A honey finish makes the cabinets in this U-shape kitchen shine. The built-in desk, television, and freestanding dinette help create a relaxed family gathering place. Designer: Connie Edwards, CKD. Cabinets: Timberlake. Appliances: GE. Sink and faucet: Blanco.

L-SHAPE PLAN

Right: Black pearl solid surfacing counters are dressed up even more with a brass towel bar on the island. The pine cabinets, range hood, and blue plaid fabrics warm the space up. Designer: Thomas D. Kling, CKD. Cabinets: Wood-Mode. Countertops: DuPont Corian. Towel bar: Mepla.

RICH CHERRY

This stunning kitchen has cherry cabinets and crown molding. Varying patterns of backsplash tile and wallcoverings add interest and complement the room's traditional decor.
Designer: Ted Langenfeld.

FOCUS ON SIMPLICITY

One element shared by every Shaker kitchen is the look of simplicity. The plan may be packed with top-notch appliances and multiple work centers, but the ambience remains somewhat reserved. Shaker looks are warmly inviting, even as they stay focused on clean straight lines and organization.

This kitchen is a perfect example of high-tech Shaker. It's filled with modern conveniences, including two separate food preparation areas, a breakfast bar, and the latest appliance technology. The up-to-the-minute workspace is embraced by simple, uncluttered-looking cabinets in the Shaker style. Here, contemporary convenience and a century-old philosophy team up to create an attractive, highly efficient kitchen.

OUTSIDE DOOR

Above: French doors connect the maple kitchen to the patio in the homeowners' yard. Designer: Toni Nolder. Cabinets: SieMatic.

DOUBLE DUTY

Left: Primary and secondary food prep areas are one big advantage of this kitchen. It's loaded with nice features, including butcher block on both sides of the range and an undercabinet refrigerator. Butcher block: John Boos & Co. Sinks: Franke.

BREAKFAST BAR

Right: The plan's main double-bowl sink is set in a green marble counter that overhangs on the other side of the island to create a dining counter. The cabinets' simple recessed panels are echoed in the framed French doors. Doors: Andersen.

A SYMPHONY IN BUTTERNUT AND BLUE

Whether you use two wood stains or go for a mix of wood and paint, combining finishes can add a lot of visual interest to a kitchen. If you're not inclined to pick up a paintbrush and work some magic yourself, you're in luck. Custom manufacturers can do the work for you. This kitchen teams blue accents on cabinet doors with a rustic-looking butternut finish.

The plan is filled with old-fashioned charm that's brought up to date with numerous modern conveniences. Glass-front cabinets and exposed storage, like the open plate rack and wood display for hanging pots, keep interesting kitchenware in full view and add to the room's homey feel. Special features, including a pull-out recycling center and cutlery divider, are ideal for keeping interiors organized—a characteristic of Shaker kitchens.

STORAGE PLUS

Above: Colorful ceramics and dinnerware are out in the open in this cherry cupboard. The plate rack rests comfortably upon five apothecary drawers. Designer: Jean Schanker, CKD. Interior Designer: Barbara Leoncavallo.

BUILT-INS

Left: Pantries are dropped back to expose some countertop space. The doors on one cabinet open to reveal a mini baking center, complete with mixer and ceramic canisters. Appliances: KitchenAid.

DINING IN

Right: Clean lines and country cabinets give this kitchen its Shaker style. A center island offers a casual spot for two people to enjoy a light meal. Cabinets: Dura Supreme. Countertops: Wilsonart. Sink: Franke.

SHAKER PRACTICALITY

You can have the best appliances and the snazziest cabinets, but if you don't have ample work surfaces, your new kitchen will come up short. Ideally, there should be counterspace for a general food prep area and for every task-related product: sink, cooktop, oven, and refrigerator. These two kitchens offer plenty of counters for all phases of mealtime. True to Shaker design principles, they are extremely functional.

A large island and an extra sink become secondary food preparation areas in both kitchens. The rooms are filled with Shaker-style cabinets offering simple designs and hardware. Open displays, including old-fashioned hooks in the kitchen on the right, mix with solid cabinets for storage. Handcrafted decorations, such as woven chair backs, add more Shaker style to spaces carefully designed with function in mind.

WORKSPACES

A stainless steel counter surrounding the gas cooktop won't warp when hot pots are placed on it. Behind the island, butcher block and a second sink make additional workspace. Designer: Harry Haynes.

CLASSIC LOOKS

From its replica vintage sink and faucet to the separate ovens and tiered work island, this Shaker kitchen is filled with practical ideas that never go out of style. Designer: John Troxell. Cabinets: Wood-Mode. Vent hood: Vent-A-Hood. Cooktop: Creda. Ovens: AEG.

A PLACE FOR EVERYTHING

Organization is one of the principal attributes of Shaker designs. The style incorporates traditional products, clean lines, and an uncluttered appearance. Organization is the key to this look, which is often achieved with plenty of cabinets to keep kitchenware off the counters.

This beautiful kitchen is a vision in white. The heavy furniture-like quality of the island, complete with cooktop, puts it at the center of attention. Sleek chairs pull up for dining in the kitchen. White tiles on the counters and backsplash run in straight rows for a clean-cut look. The kitchen design is without visual interruption. Abundant drawers and cabinets, including specialized storage space (such as plate racks), promote the open, simple Shaker style.

SIMPLE LINES

Left: The cabinets, as well as their gold door hardware, are aligned in perfect rows for design harmony.

CENTER ISLAND

Right: Simple chairs and traditional styling on the cooking/dining island are elements of Shaker design. The totally white kitchen looks crisp and orderly.

CLUTTER-FREE GOOD LOOKS

Today's Shaker kitchens are designed to reflect early 19th-century philosophies. Hallmarks of the Shaker style are clean surfaces and simple wood designs executed with superb craftsmanship. This kitchen embodies both principles.

Creamy painted walls create a smooth backdrop. The light and medium finished cherry cabinets are simple in design and beautifully crafted. The white countertops are clean and bright, blending harmoniously with earthy tile around the cooktop. Exposed shelves and hanging rails are reminiscent of kitchens from bygone days.

Natural sunlight fills the space with warmth and cheer. Below the large window, a second sink and expanse of snowy countertop offers an out-of-the-way food prep area.

EXTRA STORAGE

Above: Kitchen cabinets are built in with furniture-quality good looks. The hutch and desk are made from the same cherry wood, but finished with light and dark stains.

IN THE OPEN

Right: Exposed storage around the cooktop and vent hood keeps things organized, while providing visual interest. Colorful resilient flooring inlays create a carpet-like design. Floor: Armstrong.

SHAKER STYLE

Opposite: With its cherry cabinets customized to fit snugly, this kitchen looks neat and tailored. Designer: John Troxell. Cabinets: Wood-Mode.

BUILT TO LAST

At first glance, these two kitchens look very different; in reality, both are based on Shaker design principles of function and space. The designs are open, well-defined, and orderly.

A black-and-white motif turns the kitchen on the right into a modern Shaker variation. Natural light fills the spacious room with warmth. The kitchen chairs, complete with checkerboard motif, are all Shaker.

A more old-fashioned look is present in the kitchen below. Maple wood cabinets are clean-lined and free from ornate decoration. In the center of the kitchen, a freestanding table offers a convenient work center.

FOOD PREP

Below: With a sink nearby, this freestanding island offers a complete work center topped with butcher block. It was painted to complement the antique stove. Designer: Jim Williamson. Cabinets: Rutt.

SHAKER CHAIRS

Right: A checkerboard pattern and clean lines of painted black wood team up on the kitchen chairs. The open and organized design is contemporary Shaker. Designer: Jeffrey Boerner. Cabinets: Rutt.

Above: Rounding the end segment of counters and shelves softens the entryway into an adjoining breakfast room. Designer: Quintessentials by Mark Rosenhaus, CKD. Cabinets: Brookhaven.

A TIMELESS TREASURE

Checkerboard patterns have never gone out of style. In fact, they've become more popular in recent years as kitchens have become whiter. In this kitchen, the striking black and white squares are ideal for adding dash and interest to the floor and backsplash. Traditional white cabinets fit into any decor; teamed with the checkerboard backsplash and floor, they give the room its retro look.

A number of design features liven up this corridor kitchen. Natural light and recessed cans brighten the room. The glass-front cabinets are instrumental in keeping the design open. Exposed storage, including the curved shelves, allows subtle colorful touches to flow into the white kitchen. With checkerboard fun and a retro touch, a potentially ordinary corridor kitchen has been turned into an appealingly upbeat space.

CORRIDOR LAYOUT

Left: Crisp white countertops and traditional cabinetry turn this narrow kitchen into a bright and airy space. The open displays are less confining than solid doors. Solid surfacing: DuPont Corian.

BOLD ACCENTS

Right: Alternating squares of black and white add zest to this all-white kitchen. The checkerboard pattern evokes memories of years past while complementing today's fresh looks.

FROM DAYS GONE BY

Even old kitchens can be made to look as good as new with a facelift. This is an option worth considering if you want to revive your kitchen but your budget is tight. To get more life out of tired-looking appliances and fixtures, hire a specialist to refinish them. The kitchen on these pages was given a new lease on life through refinishing and redecorating.

From its tin ceiling to the wood plank floor, this kitchen is nostalgic and filled with charm. Wood beaded paneling covers imperfections on the walls and enhances the room's farmhouse appeal. New trim and molding complete the look. The homeowners had the sink refinished to make it shine like new. The tall cupboard was painted and stenciled to blend with the room's decor. Even the antique wood stove, which is primarily for decoration, was refinished to glossy perfection. If remodeling isn't in the cards for you, take this kitchen as an example of what you can do with some well-planned redecorating.

EXTRA STORAGE

A strawberry motif, adapted from the tablecloth, adds a lighthearted look to the painted cupboards. The kitchen showcases many classic ceramic pieces. Cupboard: Kirsch. Paints: Red-Devil.

FARMHOUSE CHARM

The century-old kitchen is freshened up with a new tin ceiling, wood floor, and beaded paneled walls. The large sink and wood-burning stove were refinished.
Designer: Charles Riley. Tin ceiling: Abbingdon Affiliates. Light fixture: Rejuvenation. Paneling: Georgia-Pacific. Fabric: Greeff.

SODA FOUNTAIN FANTASY

Theme kitchens can be a lot of fun. This design revisits trends of the 1950s, with a modern twist. The spacious kitchen flows around a boomerang island that recalls counters decorated with the popular shape decades ago. Aqua striped walls provide a lively backdrop. Another highlight is the informal eating area created with solid surfacing and backlit glass block. Fifties-style stools add a classic touch. This golden oldie is designed for the contemporary family!

COOKING CENTER

Left: Classic styling gives this range timeless appeal. The angled set-up provides plenty of counterspace on either side. *Appliances: Jenn-Air.*

CENTER ISLAND

Left: A double strip in the speckled solid surfacing top accentuates the island's boomerang shape. *Designers: John A. Buscarello, ASID, and Gail C. Olsen, CKD. Stylist: Pamela Abrahams.*

EATING IN

Above: An old-fashioned soda fountain is updated in this solid surfacing and glass-block dining area. Four brightly covered stainless stools fit comfortably. *Countertops: Wilsonart. Television: RCA.*

FIFTIES DECOR

Striking colors and patterns, from the checkerboard backsplash to the scattered floor squares, play up the crisp white cabinets. The vinyl floor is decorated with bold inlays. Tile: Florida Tile. Floor: Armstrong. Cabinets: Plain & Fancy.

STEPPING BACK IN TIME

There's something very warm and familiar about old-fashioned styling in kitchens. Somehow it conjures up images of baking fresh bread, making preserves, and doing those things nobody seems to have time for anymore. You might not have the space to include all the features this kitchen does, but even one or two classic pieces can help you evoke comforting memories of grandmother's kitchen.

Sheer window curtains let some sunlight into the space; classic ceiling fixtures provide the only other light. The metal plate stand is a great conversation piece and it makes dinnerware easily accessible. The most interesting piece, though, is the classic icebox. It's put to use as an oversized storage space. In a retro kitchen, treasured heirlooms like this one can be given completely new functions and a whole new lease on life.

EATING IN

Left: A traditional table set close to the antique stove and new buffet creates an image of years past. Light details, including the resilient floor and sheer curtains, are timeless. Floor: Armstrong.

CLASSIC PIECES

Right: A light border and floral wallcovering designs were selected to complement the vintage icebox. It's been restored to look like new and offers an interesting spot to store dinnerware and table linens. Designer: Motif Designs. Wallcovering: Motif Designs.

CRAFTED WITH FLAIR

Vibrant colors and rich textures are staples of Southwestern kitchens. Woods are often stained to show off their natural grain. Furniture pieces replace traditional built-in cabinetry.

Both kitchens featured here use furniture and open shelving to showcase bright cookware and ceramics. The hutches are multifunctional—working nicely as everyday storage and buffets for entertaining.

Windows warm the spaces with natural light. The color schemes are muted, almost aged. Decorative accents, such as the floral window treatment, carved chairs, and painted greenery on walls, add a handcrafted flavor to the designs.

BUFFET AREA

Above: Wood shelving shows off an interesting array of cookware and ceramics. The antique pine sideboard is multifunctional—offering both storage and a comfortable counter for food and drinks when company arrives. Designer: John C. Everage and Krista Everage. Sideboard: The Blue House.

ADDING SPICE

Left: This breakfast room blossoms with color. Chair backs and the bird's nest chandelier add rich, homey detailing. The freestanding display and storage hutch blends with the kitchen's natural decor. Designer: Pat Robinson, ASID. Architect: Russ Barto, AIA. Styling: Donna Pizzi. Table and chairs: Juhasz Design and Manufacturing. Chandelier: Unique Lamps.

GOURMET KITCHEN

Professional appliances suit the homeowners' culinary interests. The mood is lightened by hand-painted walls, open display areas, and the butcher-block work table. *Tile counters and floor pavers: La France. Cabinets: Hartmark Finewood Design. Refrigerator and freezer: Traulsen.*

BLENDING WOODS

Two-tone kitchens are not only becoming more popular, they're also becoming more interesting. Using one color on wall cabinets and another on base cabinets immediately gives the designer greater creative freedom.

In this kitchen, the design starts with natural maple and faux painted cabinets. Steps are echoed throughout the design. Three levels of cabinets descend on one side of the refrigerator. The floor tiles are creatively planned to overlap in steplike fashion.

Patterned glass keeps the look open, yet restricts the view inside the cabinets somewhat. Counters are all granite, but the backsplash is tile. A granite overhang on the island becomes an informal dining area. The wooden chairs add a whimsical Southwest accent.

FOOD PANTRY

Above right: Extra storage for canned goods and other items is found within this spacious painted pantry. Maple cabinets: Banks Design.

STEPPED DESIGN

Right: Wall cabinets are arranged in steplike fashion for aesthetic pleasure and convenience. Less frequently used items are up the highest. Everyday dishes are stored on lower shelves. Refrigerator: Sub-Zero. Microwave: GE.

STICKS & STONE

Left: Log chairs pull up to the granite countertop. The brick-colored tile, island seating, and soft mixed wood tones give this kitchen a Southwest flair. Designer: Cynthia Kasper. Architect: Linda Banks.

MATERIAL MIX

Above: The highly polished range hood adds a shiny metallic surface to a design that includes two woods, granite, and tile. Hood: Vent-A-Hood. Range: Magic Chef.

BACK ON THE FARM

Painstaking attention to detail is the key to this new kitchen's nostalgic charm. It's filled with soft wood tones and unusual accessories. A special finishing process lets the pine floor's knots and natural imperfections show through. The countertops and backsplash are covered with rustic hand-painted green tiles

Storage galore can be found in the casual room. Open shelving and glass fronts turn the walls into a massive display case for everything from festive dinnerware to the homeowners' collection of sand pails. The beaded cabinet doors are reminiscent of a farmhouse kitchen.

To add workspace and a casual spot for quick meals, the homeowners selected a freestanding island. Rope backsplash trim and wood ceiling beams complete the Southwestern decor.

PULL-OUTS

Left: Wicker baskets on sliding shelves hold linens and silverware. Butcher-block provides an ideal landing spot for cooking utensils and an extra food prep area. Range: Viking. Counter tile: Zone. Rope trim: Ann Sacks Tile & Stone. Baskets: Pier 1 Imports.

OPEN SHELVES

Open displays of colorful dinnerware and vintage sand pails put intriguing shapes and colors in view. The work island can be relocated for added convenience. *Designer: Carol Fox, ASID. Architect: Ketzel and Goodman. Butcher-block table and chairs: Williams-Sonoma.*

CELEBRATION OF COLOR

Like a Mexican fiesta, this kitchen is bursting with vivid color and an abundance of energy. Mosaic tile covers the walls from top to bottom. This kitchen was transformed during a major renovation from a dull rectangular plan to this one-of-a-kind showstopper. The look is now striking Southwest.

Wood ceiling beams and pine custom cabinetry are traditional Southwestern design elements. An extended run of wall cabinets showcases decorative ceramic dishes while doubling as a colorful wine rack. And everywhere, the vibrant mosaic tiles give the kitchen a vivacious feel.

Although space is limited, the angled layout fits in all the necessities. A stainless commercial-style range anchors one corner. In another, the neo-angle sink makes the wraparound windows a natural fit. This kitchen delights the eye while fulfilling the needs of the dedicated chef.

WORK TRIANGLE

Left: An angled layout keeps floor space wide open and the refrigerator, range, and sink easily accessible. A work triangle without interruptions is an integral part of a successful kitchen design. Refrigerator: Sub-Zero. Range: Wolf. Sink: Kohler. Dishwasher: KitchenAid.

ON DISPLAY

Right: A custom display case for glassware and Southwestern ceramics was created with pine wall cabinetry. Up to eight bottles of wine can be stored in ceramic drain pipes tucked behind mosaic tiles. Designer: Julie Vagts, ASID, CID. Cabinets: Wood-Mode.

WARM, WONDERFUL GREEN

You can work wonders in your kitchen by trying something a little different. A fresh coat of paint on cabinetry and wood trim can transform a simple design into one that's above the ordinary.

Here, the green cabinets are a nice contrast to the white tile countertops and backsplashes. The cabinets' flat and square recessed panels have a strongly traditional feel to balance the bright color. The cabinet interiors are peach, resulting in a Southwest-accented color scheme that complements the glassware and china stored within.

Design meets practicality to make this attractive room a great family kitchen. Open shelves keep cookbooks within reach of the cooktop and food preparation area. The natural Southwest aura is taken a step further with the wood-like resilient floor that's durable and easy to clean. A large pantry allows plenty of storage space for nonperishables. It all goes to show what you can do when you add a colorful touch to a simple, practical layout.

DOUBLE OVEN

Above: A double oven is a great idea in any kitchen. The white appliances and counter-tops stand out amidst the green custom cabinets. Cabinets: Pico Cabinet & Contracting, Inc.

BUILT-IN PANTRY

Left: Creamy peach brings a Southwestern splash to the cabinet interiors. What kitchen wouldn't benefit from organized storage in a large pantry?

STORAGE GALORE

Right: Two straight runs of cabinets meet with a corner lazy Susan, which puts canned foods and other staples close to the cooktop. Natural light floods the room through a greenhouse window. Designer: Synne Hansen, ISID. Stylist: Donna Pizzi. Sink: Kohler. Faucet: KWC.

A NATURAL FIT

An elaborate brick work center and wine storage area sets this Southwestern design in motion. The brick wall, complete with terra cotta pipes for holding wine, was part of the original plan. It was kept intact during a recent remodeling, but updated with a new double wall oven and tall pantry.

The room's color scheme is subtly Southwestern. White tile is handsomely dressed up with scattered mosaic squares and ceramic roping. Painted wall moldings and trim are lively traditional details.

The floor's darker stain is a nice contrast to the light cabinets. Another interesting decoration is featured above the sink. Here, three large windows mimic the custom cabinets' intricate glass and wood framework. In the floor and windows, as in the rest of the kitchen, the emphasis on natural materials gives the room its warm, inviting look.

BUILT-IN FEATURES

Left: Glass-front cabinets show off their contents while complementing the window designs. Cabinet panels on the refrigerator give the kitchen a sleek appearance. Cabinets: Studi Beckermann. Refrigerator: Sub-Zero. Windows: Pella.

BRICK WORKS

Right: Terra cotta pipes are arranged horizontally to hold more than 50 bottles of wine. Above the niche, a brick counter can be used to cool bread fresh out of the oven. Designer: David Jensen. Double oven: Dacor.

CENTER ISLAND

Above: An extended tile countertop becomes a breakfast bar for two. The island's gas cooktop is surrounded by ample storage and tile workspace. Tile: Pewabic. Cooktop: Dacor.

TWO FOR THE TWO-STEP

It's not always easy to pin down exactly what makes a Southwest-style kitchen. More often than not, Southwest kitchens boast one-of-a-kind designs. The two kitchens featured here take very different paths to the same point: a Southwestern look.

Traditional white cabinets with inset panels are the starting point for both rooms. Western accents, like a built-in plate rack and hammered hardware, set the tone for the kitchen below. The gingham wallcoverings, tin cookware, and beaded ceiling add up-to-date farmhouse charm.

Wood is the focal point of the kitchen on the right. It's used on the floors, windows, built-in dinette, and counters. The copper hood and quaint tiles evoke fine Southwest craftsmanship.

INTEGRAL SINK

Left: Fluted panels accent the angled counter and double-bowl solid surfacing sink. Decorative details, like the blue check backsplash, candlelight fixture, and beaded ceiling, create a down-home feeling throughout this cozy kitchen. Designer: Giorgi Kitchens. Stylist: Kathi Kermes. Cabinets: Heritage. Countertops: DuPont Corian.

COOK CENTER

Right: The restaurant-style range is surrounded by warm accents. A handcrafted look distinguishes the sweeping copper range hood, copper cookware display, and painted tiles. Designer: Mary Lynn Rockwell, CKD. Cabinets: Wm. Ohs. Hood: Vent-A-Hood.

KITCHEN WITH A HISTORY

When it came time to remodel this charming kitchen, the designers began by looking back. The original kitchen was built by Josias Joesler, a popular architect in the Southwest during the 1930s. The present designers' goal was to create a space that was fresh and new, while retaining some of its 1930s character.

Mint trim gives the traditional sandy pine cabinets a Southwestern flair. Ornate molding around the cabinets ties the new kitchen into its past. Additional Southwest accents are found in the muted tile backsplash and separate built-in hutch. The hutch's display area includes open shelves, plate racks, and old-fashioned narrow drawers.

Modern lighting helps bring this historic space into the present. Cove and undercabinet task lighting make the work spaces bright and easy to use. The result: Past and present blend harmoniously, combining classic Southwestern appeal with up-do-date convenience.

UPDATED CLASSIC

Above left: An arched door leads the way into this remodeled kitchen that preserves many elements of its original 1930s design. Designers: Elizabeth Spengler, ASID, and Jody Costan, ASID.

EXTRA STORAGE

Left: Classic trim stands tall on both sides of this recessed hutch. Cabinets are lightly finished to make them look slightly weathered and highlight the natural grain. Cabinets: Wood-Mode.

BUILT-IN FEATURES

Right: A pull-away serving cart is disguised as a typical base cabinet. On the opposite side of the U-shape plan, a spacious refrigerator is covered with panels and surrounded by meticulous woodworking to give it a classic look.

TILE, ADOBE STYLE

There's nothing like tile to dress up a kitchen and give it personality. Whether you go with a two-tone backsplash, a painted mural behind the cooktop, or something more elaborate on the walls, you can easily make a statement with tile. In this kitchen, the colors, textures, and design of the tiles impart a muted Southwestern charm.

Detailed tilework should be surrounded by less intricate materials. Here, a granite countertop complements the wall's oasis colors. White cabinets are refreshing and simple. Anything more decorative would have been distracting, possibly even overbearing. Twig drawer pulls add the final lighthearted touch.

EATING AREA

Left: Rattan furniture and a traditional hutch fit into the kitchen's neutral color scheme, while creating a slightly eclectic look overall. Designer: Robert Endres.

WORKSPACE

Right: The undermount double-bowl sink and cooktop are ideal for preparing fajitas and other Southwestern dishes. Mixed and matched wall tiles, all in hues of sand and clay, are arranged to resemble adobe structures. Tile design: Carolyn Wilson and Rick Prucker.

A PINCH OF SPICE

It's not surprising that Southwest kitchens are so popular. To begin with, their designs are timeless. Wood and tile, which are used in nearly all such kitchens, never go out of style. Southwest accents also pay tribute to nature, especially in color schemes and finishes. Woods are finished to show off their natural grain. Floors often have a slightly lived-on look.

On top of all their other attributes, Southwestern designs can be a lot of fun. Take a traditional kitchen, dress it up with zesty Southwestern patterns and colors, and you have a whole new look!

Each of the kitchens showcased here has a taste to call its very own. Notice all the wood used throughout. Tile floors, always very popular in Southwest kitchens, are relatively simple. Two of the three kitchens show off striking range hoods.

COOKING AREA

Above: Even subtle accents of color, like the tile painting shown here, add zest to light cabinets and countertops. Ventilation is provided by an adobe-like range hood. Designer: Julie Vagts. Cabinets: Wood-Mode. Liner and blower: Vent-A-Hood.

BREAKFAST BAR

Right: At least four woven chairs can fit comfortably at this large arched island. The room is filled with Southwest ambience. Notice the bold throw rug, wood ceiling beams, and lively backsplash. Designer: Cailin M. Thelen, CKD, CBD. Architect: Kenneth J. Thelen, CKD, AIA. Cabinets: Mouser Kitchens.

RANGE HOOD

A striking geometric pattern makes the range hood this kitchen's focal point. The design, which is duplicated on the backsplash, is softened by rustic floor tiles and natural wood cabinets. *Designer: Kitchens & Baths by Louise. Range: Wolf.*

GRAND LIVING SPACE

A kitchen that flows into adjoining living space is ideal for both entertaining and everyday use. Such a layout keeps the hub of family activity centered in one area of the home. An open view brings everyone together, even though separate activities and conversations may be taking place.

This sunny design centers on an extended U-shape run of kitchen cabinets and counters. On one end, a glass table is used for dining. The portion that faces the family room includes a cooktop, stools for gathering, and a wet bar. An oversize refrigerator anchors the arrangement.

The kitchen is filled with desirable features. Ample storage keeps counters clutter free. A built-in desk makes meal planning and household organization easy. There's even a separate recycling island. A wall of glass windows adds natural brightness and delightful views. Family members can get the most out of spending time together in this delightful space.

WITH A VIEW

Left: The open layout lets the kitchen and adjoining family room flow as one, although custom cabinetry doubles as a room divider. Rows of windows let the sun shine in. *Designer: Jackie Naylor Interiors, Inc. Countertops: DuPont Corian. Tile floor: Zumpano.*

WORK TRIANGLE

Right: With the main sink, refrigerator, and cooktop each easily accessible from the others, this kitchen is both practical and appealing. A recycling island is out of view behind the refrigerator. *Pendant light: Lightolier. Cabinets: New-Age Cabinets. Refrigerator: Sub-Zero. Cooktop: Thermador.*

ISLANDS IN THE STREAM

Below: There's seating for eight at this creative L-shape island. The mix of glass block and black counters is striking and elegant. Designer: Ayeshah Morin. Glass blocks: Pittsburgh Corning. Refrigerator: Sub-Zero.

You're lucky if there's room for an island in your kitchen. Used for food preparation, cooking, or as informal eating areas, islands play an important role in today's kitchens. The owners of this contemporary gem are blessed with not just one, but two, islands.

The first is an oval workspace that includes a built-in gas cooktop. There's lots of storage space below for large skillets and a wok, in addition to other cooking essentials. A second island dramatically combines glass block and solid surfacing. The L-shape includes seating for eight and acts as a buffer between the kitchen and adjoining space.

When it comes to islands in your kitchen (if you have enough room), designers say, the more the merrier!

BLACK & WHITE

Pure white cabinets free of knobs and pulls teamed with glossy black accents turn this kitchen into a modern masterpiece. The marble tile floor and sunroom windows complete the bold, contemporary look.

LET THE SUNSHINE IN

So often kitchens are thought of as little boxes or rectangles—four walls, a window, and a couple of doors in and out. But kitchens can be transformed into more interesting shapes. And there's no rule that says kitchens must have any walls at all!

This kitchen does away with the four-walled box. Its layout is set with an angled run of cabinets overlooking a casual living area. Sun flows right through the exterior windows of the home into the open kitchen. Bleached wood cabinets and a hazy blue tile backsplash are a natural fit. The custom cabinets, beveled to match wainscotting on nearby walls, unify the kitchen and adjoining space. Butcher-block work surfaces are handy for food preparation, and black appliances and open storage areas lend an interesting contrast. This well-designed space certainly doesn't suffer for its lack of walls.

NATURAL LOOKS

Above: A refreshing variety of colors and materials complement each other. Blue tile is a bright backdrop for traditional bleached doors. The butcher-block counter is hardworking and neutral.

GREAT ROOM

Right: A creative cabinet arrangement works as a partial room divider between the kitchen and family room. It also allows sunlight to stream into the kitchen from the extended glass windows. Cooktop: Thermador.

FOOD PREP

Left: A raised ledge behind the cooking area lets the cook converse with guests, while keeping the food preparation out of view. Designer: John A. Buscarello. Refrigerator: GE.

A SUNROOM SOLUTION

You can recognize a California/Florida kitchen by its sunny design. Natural light flows in through numerous, usually oversized windows. Surfaces and cabinets are light in color and often contemporary in style. But very few kitchens are anywhere near as bright as the one showcased here.

With walls made of glass, this kitchen looks like a natural extension of the well-groomed yard. Base storage, like that used in restaurants, gives the room a commercial appeal that's well suited to the kitchen's made-for-entertaining design. The floor is hardworking tile, perfect for the outdoor setting. Tall hedges planted around the yard provide some privacy.

The owners of this kitchen have the best of both the indoor and outdoor worlds. Every meal becomes a picnic sheltered from wind and weather, just steps away from a well-appointed kitchen.

FOOD PREP AREA

Left: A durable butcher-block counter makes a safe cutting, mixing, and blending spot. It's conveniently placed next to the commercial range. Design: Four Seasons Greenhouse. Range: Vulcan.

EATING IN

Right: A rattan dinette fits right in with its summery surroundings. Additional seating can be created with stools pulled up to the extended countertop. The open design is ideal for garden parties.

SPACE-ENHANCING LAYOUTS

Typical kitchen floor plans can be dramatically transformed by shapely runs of cabinetry. These two sunny kitchens are good examples of how creative arrangements can be big on both style and function.

Cabinets wrap around glass walls almost playfully in the kitchen below. The result is a spacious walkway and a design filled with storage. There's room for an island, complete with informal seating and workspace. The bleached cabinets, metallic range hood, and clean white countertops add to the kitchen's relaxed ambience.

In the kitchen on the right, a peninsula is extended for several purposes: The informal space needs the extra storage the extension offers, built-in cubicles for wine are an added plus, and the angled peninsula also separates an eating area from the main hub of kitchen activity. Gray and white tiles used throughout the room keep the look light and breezy.

COUNTER APPEAL

Below: A sweeping cabinet layout adds plenty of storage and counterspace to this kitchen with a view. Designer: Terri Salazar. Cabinets: Heritage Custom Kitchens.

FOOD PREP

Shades of gray and white give the space a carefree contemporary look. The angled peninsula can be used for cutting up vegetables or serving food. Designer: Shirley Anderson, CKD. Cabinets: Dura Supreme. Tile: American Olean. Oven and cooktop: Dacor. Vent hood: Vent-A-Hood.

CLASSICAL PERFECTION

Details borrowed from classical architecture can work wonders in dressing up a kitchen. The designers of these two neoclassic spaces used finely crafted wooden columns to bring a taste of tradition to their new plans.

Double columns and a light valance add a formal look to the sink and casual dining space in the kitchen on the left. Wall cabinets are jagged for interest. A classic arch hovers above the double oven and pantry area. Molding throughout is painted to stand out from the cabinets.

The island in the kitchen on the right is a showstopper. Four columns frame the elaborate workspace, complete with built-in cooktop. The cabinets and hardwood floor are naturally finished to highlight the wood's grain.

PRIMARY SINK

Left: While keeping the updated kitchen open to an adjoining room, two columns and a custom light valance frame the stainless sink. Vintage-style cabinets are accented with neoclassic glass designs and painted molding. Design: Maria Weingard and John Brandon. Oven: KitchenAid. Cabinets: Rutt.

WOOD BEAUTY

Right: An ornate relief pattern dresses up the area above the built-in microwave oven. The new traditional-style cabinets are complemented by the polished hardwood floor.

CENTER ISLAND

Above: Four columns turn this center island into a freestanding piece of furniture. The ornate chandelier is supplemented by recessed and natural light. Designers: John Baronowski and Smith Baron. Cabinets: Yorktowne.

MADE FOR A CHEF

Even if a kitchen is filled with commercial-style equipment and professional-caliber work stations, the design doesn't have to be cold. The kitchen shown here is filled with finely crafted details that make the space warm and inviting. It's evident that the homeowner chef who uses his hands to create gourmet dishes appreciates handmade good looks in his surroundings.

An exquisite leaded glass window in the Arts and Crafts style is the centerpiece of the floor plan. The window's colors and molding are picked up elsewhere in the room. Cherry cabinets have a fiery finish that highlights their natural grain and simple design. The billowy colors on the floor and backsplash tile lend another handcrafted detail.

The island adds more work space and a second sink. Its raised expanse of butcher block can be used for informal dining, preparing meals, or presenting a buffet. The extra sink is conveniently placed just feet from the commercial range.

HANDY PULL-OUT

Above: A pull-out cutting board maximizes space in any kitchen. Here it offers a convenient spot for cutting vegetables before tossing them into the wok. Wok: Garland.

FOR THE GOURMET

Right: The serious cook will appreciate the commercial appliances and variety of workspaces this plan offers. Cabinets: Wood-Mode. Range: Garland.

STAINED GLASS

Right: Colors and finishes used throughout the kitchen were selected to complement the artisan window. The window design was inspired by the work of Frank Lloyd Wright. Designer: John Troxell. Refrigerator: Sub-Zero.

RESOURCE DIRECTORY

DESIGNERS & ARCHITECTS

Abbey's Kitchens & Baths, Inc.
685 Broadway
Bayonne, NJ 07002

Shirley Anderson, CKD
Kitchens & Baths by Shirley
1301 Court St.
Redding, CA 96001

Gae Aulenti
Snaidero International
201 W. 132nd St.
Los Angeles, CA 90061

Sheron Bailey, CKD
Design Ideas
12390 Avenue 18½
Chowcilla, CA 93610

Linda Banks
Banks Design
175 W. Norwalk Rd.
Norwalk, CT 06850

John Baronowski
Smith Baron
800 Perry Highway
Suite 4
Pittsburgh, PA 15229

Jeffrey Boerner
Artistic Furnishings, Inc.
30 W. Brad St.
Box 598
Trumbaursville, PA 18970

Michael J. Boyette, CKD
Boyette Kitchens & Baths
214 Montgomery St.
Bloomfield, NJ 07003

John A. Buscarello, ASID
1 University Place #9-0
New York, NY 10003

Cecilia Campa
Becker Zeyco Kitchens
Sobel Design Bldg.
680 Eigth St.
Suite 169A
San Francisco, CA 94103

Rina Cohen, MDIA
Rina Cohen Interiors
Suite 1
649 Inkerman Rd.
Caulfield North
Australia 3161

Mark Combs
Crestwood, Inc.
353 East Avenue A
Salina, KS 67401

Connie Edwards, CKD
American Woodmark
3102 Shawnee Dr.
Winchester, VA 22601

Maxwell Eisenberg
1942 Delancey St.
Philadelphia, PA 19103

Beverly Ellsley
175 Post Rd. West
Westport, CT 06880

Steven P. Emerson
Kitchens of Distinction
6719 Seybold Rd.
Madison, WI 53719

Robert Endres
Perlmutter & Freiwald
P.O. Box 250576
Franklin, MI 48025

Everage Design Alliance
909 Lucille Ave.
Venice, CA 90291

Linda Ferry
Architectural Illumination
P.O. Box 2690
Monterey, CA 93942

Albert Fink, Ph.D., CKD
Kitchens at the Denver
639 Kalamath
Denver, CO 80204

Rita Foulk
Crestwood, Inc.
353 East Avenue A
Salina, KS 67401

Carol Fox, ASID
Carol Fox Designs
1293 Calle De Madrid
Pacific Palisades, CA 90272

Merrie Fredericks
Design Concepts Plus
18 E. Eagle Rd.
Havertown, PA 19083

Elizabeth B. Gillin
Elizabeth B. Gillin Interiors
400 Wychwood Rd.
Westfield, NJ 07090

Giorgi Kitchens
218 Philadelphia Pike
Wilmington, DE 19809

Joan Halperin Interior Design
401 E. 80th St.
New York, NY 10021

Gary Hancock
Deborah A. Litz-Beard
Kitchens Plus
31815 W. 8 Mile Rd.
Livonia, MI 48152

Synne Hansen, IIDA
Hansen Designs
3735 Malibu Country Dr.
Malibu, CA 90265-4714

Harry Haynes, CKD
Hillcraft Design Studio
2202 Advance Rd.
Madison, WI 53704

Nancy Wall Hopkins
748 55th St.
Des Moines, IA 50312

Bob Howering
Baker Woodcraft
Route 206 Box 502
Flanders, NJ 07836

Candace Ihlenfeldt
Brit Goldstine
The Showplace, Inc.
8710 Willows Rd.
P.O. Box 955
Redmond, VA 98073-0955

David Jensen
Kitchens by Jensen, Inc.
563 S. Eton
Birmingham, MI 48009

Cynthia Kaspar, ASID
Interior Accents
43 Fairview Farm Rd. West
Redding, CT 06896

Kitchens & Baths by Louise Gil Martin
245 Vine St.
Reno, NV 89503

Thomas D. Kling, CKD
Thomas D. Kling, Inc.
2474 N. George St.
York, PA 17402

Jim Krengel, CKD, CBD, ISID
Kitchens by Krengel
1688 Grand Ave.
St. Paul, MN 55105

Kulla Kitchens
7800 Rockwell Ave.
Philadelphia, PA 19111

Ted Lagenfeld
Nebraska Custom Kitchens
4601 Dodge St.
Omaha, NE 68132

Joe LaMantia, CKD
Lynn Larsen, CKD
LaMantia Design
9100 Ogden Ave.
Brookfield, IL 60513

Patti Lawson, CKD
Michael Pachan
Dayton Showcase Co.
10915 Reading Rd.
Cincinnati, OH 45241

Susie Leader Interiors Inc.
30555 Southfield
Suite 165
Southfield, MI 48067

Barbara Leoncavallo
45 Monroe Ave.
Pittsford, NY 14534

George Magyar, CKD
Splash
244 Needham St.
Newton, MA 02164

Jane Burdette Manko
Schurman's Inc.
1 Ohio River Blvd.
Sewickley, PA 15143

William David Martin, AIA
P.O. Box 2053
Monterey, CA 93940

Sharon Matson
1231 Yosemite Blvd.
Birmingham, MI 48009

Lisa McCauley
RL Tech
220 S. Cook St.
Barrington, IL 60010

Trudy McGinnis, CKD, CBD
Brookwood Kitchens
2140 Peachtree Rd. NW
Atlanta, GA 30309

Nancy McGowen, Allied ASID
McGowen Associates
311 Walnut Blvd.
Rochester, MI 48307

Beth Mellina
835 Highland Ave.
Westfield, NJ 07090

Ayeshah Morin
Designer Kitchens Inc.
17300 E. Seventeenth St.
Suite A
Tustin, CA 92680

Motif Designs
20 Jones St.
New Rochelle, NY 10802

Nancy Mullan
204 E. 77th St.
New York, NY 10021

Anne Mullin Interiors, Inc.
189 Mason St.
Greenwich, CT 06830

Jackie Naylor, CKD, Allied ASID
Jackie Naylor Interiors, Inc.
4287 Glengary Dr., NE
Atlanta, GA 30342

Toni Nolder
Distinctive Kitchen Designs
24 Main St.
P.O. Box 297
Centerbrook, CT 06409

Gail C. Olsen, CKD
Ducci Kitchens
379 Goshen Rd.
Torington, CT 06790

Sharon Overstake, CKD
Wm. Ohs Showrooms
2900 E. Sixth Ave.
Denver, CO 80206

Designs by Florence Perchuk, Ltd.
127 E. 59th St.
Suite 201
New York, NY 10022

Pinninfarina
Snaidero International
201 W. 132nd St.
Los Angeles, CA 90061

Sharon M. Pretto, ISID
245 Steamboat Rd.
Great Neck, NY 11024

Bob Pulte
Manor Homes, Inc.
1100 N. Woodward Ave.
Suite 128
Bloomfield Hills, MI 48301

John J. Quinn II
77 Buena Vista Ave.
Rumson, NJ 07760

Quintessentials
Mark Rosenhaus, CKD
525 Amsterdam Ave.
New York, NY 10024

Sarah L. Reep
Carolyn Haney
Fieldstone Cabinetry, Inc.
P.O. Box 109
Highway 105 East
Northwood, IA 50459

Charles Riley
45 Fifth Ave, #9D
New York, NY 10003

Pat Robinson, ASID
2 Broken Bow Lane
Rolling Hills Estates, CA 90274

Mary Lynn Rockwell, CKD
Wm. Ohs Showroom
2900 E. 6th Ave.
Denver, CO 80226

Barbara Hauben Ross
Barbara Hauben Ross Interior Design
226 E. 54th St.
New York, NY 10022

Cheryl Casey Ross
6712 Colbath Ave.
Van Nuys, CA 91405

Bonnie Sachs, ASID
311 Bora Bora Way
Suite 305
Marina del Rey, CA 90293

Terri Salazar
Kitchens Del Mar
3536 E. Coast Hwy.
Corona Del Mar, CA 92625

Jean Schanker, CKD
JS Design
65 Carandon Way
Rochester, NY 14618

Alvin Schneider Design
110 Greene St.
New York, NY 10013

John J. Schneider
John J. Schneider Design
P.O. Box 1457
Pebble Beach, CA 93953

Val Siddell
Crestwood, Inc.
353 E. Avenue A
Salina, KS 67401

Michael Skott
Route 1, Box 66D
Eastsound, WA 98245

Elizabeth Spengler, ASID
Jody Costan, ASID
Dorado Designs, Inc.
4640 E. Sunrise Dr.
Tucson, AZ 85718

Dagmar Theil, CKD
Kitchen & Bath Design
2 Theater St.
Suite 307
Orinda, CA 94563

Thelen Kitchen & Bath Studios
5566 Chamblee-Dunwoody Rd.
Atlanta, GA 30338

John Troxell
Wood-Mode Cabinetry
One Second St.
Kreamer, PA 17833

Julie Vagts
The Kitchen Works
16 E. Holly St.
Pasadena, CA 91103

Diana Valentine, CKD
Brit Goldstein
The Showplace, Inc.
P.O. Box 955
Redmond, WA 98073-0955

Gary White, CKD
Kitchen & Bath Design
1000 Bristol St.
Newport Beach, CA 92660

Wendi Wilkins
Judy McCaffrey
Puff's of Petoskey
1200 Bay View Rd.
Petoskey, MI 49770

Jim Williamson
2021 E. Lynn St.
Seattle, WA 98112

SUPPLIERS

AEG/Andi-Co.
65 Campus Plaza
Edison, NJ 08837

Amana Refrigeration, Inc.
Highway 220
Amana, IA 52204

American Olean Tile Co.
1000 Cannon Ave.
Lansdale, PA 19446-0271

American Standard
1 Centennial Plaza
P.O. Box 6820
Piscataway, NJ 08855-6820

American Woodmark
3102 Shawnee Dr.
Winchester, VA 22601

Andersen Windows
P.O. Box 12
Bayport, MN 55003

Armstrong World Industries
P.O. Box 3001
Lancaster, PA 17604

Avonite
1945 Highway 304
Belen, NM 87002

Bertch Cabinet Mfg., Inc.
4747 Crestwood Dr.
Waterloo, IA 50702

Blanco America Inc.
1001 Lower Landing Rd.
Blackwood, NJ 08012

Bosch Household Products
2800 S. 25th Ave.
Broadview, IL 60513

The Broadway Collection
1010 W. Santa Fe
P.O. Box 1210
Olathe, KS 66051-1210

Brookhaven
a division of Wood-Mode
1 Second St.
Kreamer, PA 17833

Brubaker Kitchens
1121 Manheim Pike
Lancaster, PA 17601

Brunschwig & Fils
75 Virginia Rd.
North White Plains, NY 10603

Chapman House Custom Cabinetry
311 Walnut Blvd.
Rochester, MI 48307

Chicago Brass Faucet Co.
2100 S. Clearwater Dr.
Des Plaines, IL 60018

Country Floors
8735 Melrose Ave.
Los Angeles, CA 90069

Creda
5700 W. Touhy Ave.
Chicago, IL 60648

Crestwood, Inc.
353 East Avenue A
Salina, KS 67401

Crystal Cabinet Works
1100 Crystal Dr.
Princeton, MN 55391

CSC
27615 Hopkins Avenue
Valencia, CA 91355

Dacor
950 S. Raymond Ave.
Pasadena, CA 91109-7202

Dal Tile Corp.
7834 Hawn Freeway
Dallas, TX 75217

Design Line Cabinets
P.O. Box 9
Sauk Rapids, MN 56879

Downsview Cabinetry
2635 Rena Rd.
Mississauga, Ontario
Canada

DuPont Corian
1007 Market St.
Wilmington, DE 19898

Dura-Bilt Products
P.O. Box 188
Wellsburg, NY 14894

Eljer
17120 Dallas Parkway
Dallas, TX 75248

Elkay Mfg. Co.
2222 Camden Ct.
Oak Brook, IL 60521

Fieldstone Cabinetry, Inc.
P.O. Box 109
Highway 105 East
Northwood, IA 50459

Florida Tile
608 Prospect St.
Lakeland, FL 33802

Fonthill, Ltd.
578 Nepperhan Ave.
Yonkers, NY 10701

Four Seasons Sunrooms
5005 Veterans Memorial Hwy.
Holbrook, NY 11741

Franke
212 Church Rd.
Dept. H
North Wales, PA 19454

Gaggenau USA Corp.
5 Commonwealth Ave.
Woburn, MA 01801

Garland Commercial Ind., Inc.
185 E. South St.
Freeland, PA 18224

General Electric
Appliance Park
Louisville, KY 40225

Georgia-Pacific Corp.
P.O. Box 1763
Norcrow, GA 30091

Greeff
204-206 E. 58th St.
New York, NY 10022

Grohe America
241 Covington Dr.
Bloomington, IL 60108

Hallmark Cabinets
4851 Warehouse Rd.
Salt Lake City, UT 84118

Halo
400 Busse Rd.
Oak Grove Village, IL 60007

Gary Hartmark
Hartmark Finewood Design
26350 Athena Ave.
Harbor City, CA 90710

Debra Hecht
6285 Thurber Rd.
Bloomfield Hills, MI 48301

Heritage Custom Kitchens
215 Diller Ave.
New Holland, PA 17557

Hettich America
P.O. Box 7664
Charlotte, NC 28241

Hinson & Co.
27-35 Jackson Ave.
Long Island City, NY 11101

In-Sink-Erator
4700 21st St.
Racine, WI 53406-5093

Ipocork
P.O. Box 125
2211 Lithonia Industrial Blvd.
Lithonia, GA 30058

Jenn-Air Co.
3035 Shadeland
Indianapolis, IN 46226-0901

John Boos & Co.
315 S. First St.
Effingham, IL 62402

Kentile Floors, Inc.
58 Second Ave.
Brooklyn, NY 11215

Kirsch Division
Cooper Industries, Inc.
P.O. Box 370
Sturgis, MI 49091-0370

KitchenAid
2303 Pipestone Rd.
Benton Harbor, MI 49022

Kohler
444 Highland Dr.
Kohler, WI 53044

KWC
1559 Sunland Lane
Costa Mesa, CA 92626

Lightolier
100 Lighting Way
Secaucus, NJ 07096

Magic Chef Co.
740 King Edward Ave.
Cleveland, TN 37311

Maytag Co.
1 Dependability Square
Newton, IA 50208

Mepla, Inc.
909 W. Market Center Dr.
Highpoint, NC 27260

Mouser Kitchens
2102 N. Highway 31-W
P.O. Box 2527
Elizabethtown, KY 42702

Nemo Tile
48 E. 21st St.
New York, NY 10010

Nevamar Corp.
8339 Telegraph Rd.
Odenton, MD 21113

New Age Cabinets
1230 Logan Circle NW
Atlanta, GA 30318

Pella Windows & Doors
102 Main St.
Pella, IA 50219

Pewabic Pottery
10125 E. Jefferson
Detroit, MI 48214

Pico Cabinet & Contracting, Inc.
3018 Pico Blvd.
Santa Monica, CA 90405

Pier 1 Imports
P.O. Box 961020
Ft. Worth, TX 76161-0020

Pindler and Pindler
11910 Poindexter Ave.
Moorpark, CA 93102

Plain & Fancy Custom Cabinets
P.O. Box 519
Schaefferstown, PA 17088

Progress Lighting
Erie Avenue & G St.
Philadelphia, PA 19134

Quaker Maid
Route 61
P.O. Box H
Leesport, PA 19534

Quality Custom Kitchens
515 Big Stone Gap Rd.
Duncanville, TX 75317

Regal Floorcoverings
11854 Olympic Blvd.
Los Angeles, CA 90064

Russell Range, Inc.
325 S. Maple
Unit 5
South San Francisco, CA 94080

Rutt Custom Cabinetry
1564 Main St.
P.O. Box 129
Goodville, PA 17528

Rutt of Seattle
Seattle Design Center
Suite 121
5701 6th Ave. South
Seattle, WA 98108

Ann Sacks Tile & Stone
500 N.W. 23rd Ave.
Portland, OR 97210

Debbie Seymour
15 Springbrook Rd.
Morristown, NJ 07960

Snaidero International USA
201 W. 132nd St.
Los Angeles, CA 90061

Studio Shades
c/o Bonnie Sachs, ASID
Suite 305
311 Bora Bora Way
Marina del Rey, CA 90292

Sub-Zero Freezer Co., Inc.
P.O. Box 4130
Madison, WI 53744-4130

Thermador
5119 District Blvd.
Los Angeles, CA 90040

Tiffany & Co.
1414 Walnut St.
Philadelphia, PA 19102

Timberlake Cabinet Co.
a division of American Woodmark
3102 Shawnee Dr.
Winchester, VA 22601

Traulsen & Co., Inc.
11402 15th Ave.
College Point, NY 11356

U-Line
8900 N. 55th St.
Milwaukee, WI 53223

Vance Industries, Inc.
7401 W. Wilson Ave.
Chicago, IL 60656

Vent-A-Hood
P.O. Box 830426
Richardson, TX 75081

Viking Range Corp.
P.O. Box 956
Greenwood, MS 38930

Jackie Warschaw
1614 Tower Grove Dr.
Beverly Hills, CA 90210

Waverly
79 Madison Ave.
New York, NY 10016

Western Wood Products Assoc.
522 SW 5th Ave.
Portland, OR 92704

Whirlpool Corp.
2000 M63 North (MD6001)
Benton Harbor, MI 49022

Williams-Sonoma
The Pavillions
Fair Oaks Blvd.
Sacramento, CA 94825

Wilsonart
P.O. Box 6110
600 S. General Bruce Dr.
Temple, TX 76503-6110

Wm. Ohs Cabinetry, Inc.
2900 E. 6th St.
Denver, CO 60035

Wolf Range Co.
19600 S. Alameda St.
Compton, CA 90221-6291

Wood-Mode
One Second St.
Kreamer, PA 17833

Yorktowne, Inc.
100 Redco Ave.
Red Lion, PA 17356

Zone
Pacific Design Center
8687 Melrose Ave.
Los Angeles, CA 90048

Zumpano
375 Pharr Rd.
Atlanta, GA 30305